New Directions for
Higher Education

Betsy O. Barefoot
Jillian L. Kinzie
CO-EDITORS

Connecting Learning Across the Institution

Pamela L. Eddy

EDITOR

Number 165 • Spring 2014
Jossey-Bass
San Francisco

CONNECTING LEARNING ACROSS THE INSTITUTION
Pamela L. Eddy
New Directions for Higher Education, no. 165
Betsy O. Barefoot and Jillian L. Kinzie, Co-editors

Microfilm copies of issues and articles are available in 16mm and 35mm, as well as microfiche in 105mm, through University Microfilms Inc., 300 North Zeeb Road, Ann Arbor, MI 48106-1346.

NEW DIRECTIONS FOR HIGHER EDUCATION (ISSN 0271-0560, electronic ISSN 1536-0741) is part of The Jossey-Bass Higher and Adult Education Series and is published quarterly by Wiley Subscription Services, Inc., A Wiley Company, at Jossey-Bass, One Montgomery Street, Suite 1200, San Francisco, CA 94104-4594. Periodicals Postage Paid at San Francisco, California, and at additional mailing offices. POSTMASTER: Send address changes to New Directions for Higher Education, Jossey-Bass, One Montgomery Street, Suite 1200, San Francisco, CA 94104-4594.

New Directions for Higher Education is indexed in Current Index to Journals in Education (ERIC); Higher Education Abstracts.

Individual subscription rate (in USD): $89 per year US/Can/Mex, $113 rest of world; institutional subscription rate: $311 US, $351 Can/Mex, $385 rest of world. Single copy rate: $29. Electronic only–all regions: $89 individual, $311 institutional; Print & Electronic–US: $98 individual, $357 institutional; Print & Electronic–Canada/Mexico: $98 individual, $397 institutional; Print & Electronic–Rest of World: $122 individual, $431 institutional.

Editorial correspondence should be sent to the Co-editor, Betsy O. Barefoot, Gardner Institute, Box 72, Brevard, NC 28712.

Cover photograph © Digital Vision

www.josseybass.com

CONTENTS

Part III: Planning for the Future

Editor's Notes

Public demands for accountability in institutions of higher education concentrate on various definitions of student success (Bain, 2012; Pascarella & Terenzini, 2005), yet at the heart of these mandates is a focus on improved student learning. What is often missing in these debates, however, is attention to the fuller range of learning that occurs within colleges, including faculty as learners and the role of organizational learning in improving operations and processes on college campuses.

Traditionally, research on higher education occurs in silos based on stakeholder perspective. Thus, one might read an article dedicated to students as learners, another that discusses faculty as adult learners, and yet another that deals with institutional learning or community engagement. This volume seeks to break down these silos and draw together scholars who research learning from the vantage points of a variety of stakeholders in higher education institutions. The objective is to understand what is common in learning across the institution, what differs, and how concepts of learning theory from specific focal areas can expand how we think about learning in general. For example, what can faculty developers learn from the research on integration of learning among students? How does learning by faculty translate into enhanced student learning or organizational learning? How might the emerging discussion linking civic engagement by students to postsecondary access and subsequent learning outcomes of undergraduate students impact the scholarship of teaching and learning? How does research on the role of civic engagement on student learning outcomes inform thinking about organizational learning? A set of four questions framed the research presented in this volume, namely:

- What are the key issues of learning facing each stakeholder group?
- How does the integration of learning occur within and among groups of students, faculty, leaders, and the institution?
- What approaches to learning are transferable among stakeholder groups?
- How do we create an overarching theory of learning that might have multiple applications?

Learning is a cornerstone of the mission of colleges and universities. According to Kolb (1998), "most of us develop learning styles that emphasize some learning abilities over others" (p. 131). Kolb's Learning Style Inventory (LSI) identifies four types of learning styles that the model divides into quadrants to represent each style. *Accommodators, divergers, assimilators,* and *convergers* each have distinct learning preferences

New Directions for Higher Education, no. 165, Spring 2014 © 2014 Wiley Periodicals, Inc.
Published online in Wiley Online Library (wileyonlinelibrary.com) • DOI: 10.1002/he.20078

and incorporate new information in different ways. What all four of Kolb's learning styles have in common is a willingness to reflect on an experience or an idea and to apply that learning through active experimentation or well-thought-out modifications to existing processes. It is through reflection that an individual can build on his or her existing cognitive schema. Kolb's (1998) research informs how individuals learn, thus it applies to both faculty and students alike.

Mezirow (1997) focuses on learning for adults and described transformational learning in adult learners as a process of critical reflection through which one changes his or her frame of reference. Changes occur as a result of immersion in a new situation, through interactions, and from reading and gaining new information. These shifts in thinking result from the "aha" moments of life. Mezirow's (1997) typology of the four processes of learning is useful in understanding how new knowledge and experiences are incorporated. The first process of learning allows for expansion of current perspectives. The second learning process in Mezirow's typology relates to the creation of new points of view. His third learning process involves a transformation in point of view. The fourth learning process in Mezirow's typology involves an epochal change to an underlying schema. This type of learning is uncommon; more typically, an individual's underlying schema or sense of self is less malleable.

Recent work in the learning sciences focuses on deep learning (Huber & Hutchings, 2004) and adaptive expertise (Budwig, 2013). Situated learning provides opportunities for deep learning to occur through engagement and "involves the learners' gradual adoption of the practices, beliefs, and values of a specific expert community" (Budwig, 2013, p. 43). The LEAP initiative of the Association of American Colleges and Universities (see http://www.aacu.org/leap/documents/EssentialOutcomes_Chart.pdf) outlines student learning outcomes that build on development along the domains of knowledge, practice, responsibility, and integration.

Against this backdrop of the ways in which individuals learn is the concept of organizational learning. Similar to individual learning, organizational learning occurs by processing information and ultimately changing behavior (Huber, 1991). Kezar (2005) summarized, "Some of the main concepts in organizational learning are single- and double-looped learning, inquiry and action, theories-in-use, overload, and information interpretation processes such as unlearning and organizational memory (among many others)" (p. 10). As with individuals, it is important for organizations to use feedback loops to reflect on actions and consequences in order to change behavior. Knowing more about how best to intersect the concepts of individual learning and organizational learning can help inform practice within the academy.

The chapters in this volume are tied together by key themes framing research on learning theory. Investigation of the motivating factors for learning for individuals and for institutions pays particular attention to individual location along the developmental continuum of integration (Barber, 2012). A framework emerges with the compilation of the stakeholder perspectives that allows for a questioning of underlying assumptions regarding learning. By interrogation of the issues facing each stakeholder group, it is possible to highlight the barriers to connecting learning theories across silos that emerge between theoretical approaches to learning based on stakeholder location. Highlighting the differences in discussing learning based on group (i.e., students, faculty, organizations) helps to instead show areas of commonality among the learning theories typically employed to study students, faculty, and organizations. Despite the lack of common naming of terms or theories for stakeholder groups, commonality exists that allows for further advancement of thinking across and within each of these domains.

This volume of *New Directions for Higher Education* explores what it means to bridge learning across the institution. Part I of the volume provides context for the issues facing institutions regarding learning. This Editor's Notes establishes the framework regarding learning theories throughout the institution and identifies key themes in the research. Chapter 1 by Barber provides a framework for how students connect their learning using an integration of learning model. Chapter 2 presents examples of faculty as learners, focusing on how international teaching and research influenced faculty perspectives. In Chapter 3, Moore and Mendez argue that institutionalizing civic engagement enhances student success and intentionally using organizational learning processes can provide support for student learning.

Part II of the volume contains a number of case examples focusing on different stakeholder groups. Chapter 4 by Leslie uses the concept of orthogonality to showcase how stakeholders can view intersections of learning in college and how assessment of outcomes creates a framework to support learning across the college experience. In Chapter 5, Wawrzynski and Baldwin present how connected learning by students using high-impact learning opportunities contributes to student learning outcomes. They articulate how campus mapping of various learning opportunities can create intentionality regarding student learning and provide examples of how to implement this on campus. How faculty support their own learning is the focus of Chapter 6 by Zakrajsek, who argues that peer learning among faculty provides a critical on-campus resource for faculty development. Chapter 7 by VanDerLinden focuses on how blended learning can provide the foundation for strategic changes on campus, and ultimately result in organizational learning.

The last section, Part III, considers plans for the future and implications for practice. In Chapter 8, Amey provides an analysis of the overarching connections among learning theories for the various stakeholder groups. She draws links between various learning theory definitions and offers advice on how to break down existing silos to create a shared understanding of learning theories. In Chapter 9, Neumann and Bolitzer investigate how individual differences in learning and context create opportunities for creative approaches to learning. Implications for faculty are reviewed and a plan is laid out for leaders to provide the best support for a span of learners. Finally, in Chapter 10, Chance offers a synthesis of strategies to connect learning across the institution. Each chapter includes campus-based examples, offers best practices, or covers implications for practice and policy to support learning.

Throughout this volume, several key themes inform the research and writing. They include the following:

- An examination of various factors that contribute to learning for students, faculty, and organizations.
- A theoretical framework to analyze learning for and across groups of individuals and institutions.
- An examination of the underlying assumptions regarding critical factors that best scaffold learning.
- An emphasis on the influence of structure on learning.

This volume, thus, has both a scholarly and a practical bent. Professionals researching student learning, faculty development, or organizational learning will find useful takeaways. For scholars, the volume advances the knowledge about the ways we investigate and study learning across and for various groups of learners. Institutional leaders will benefit from this research as it collects thinking about learning in its various formats in one location and provides a platform for synthesis. Instead of thinking of learning as discrete depending on the stakeholder group, this volume highlights the commonalities across all types of learning. Many institutions are now undergoing various forms of curricular review to address the shifting nature of what student outcomes are desired from a college education. Similarly, faculty work is changing with new demands that push responsibilities, but the locus of work still centers on how to scaffold student learning. How faculty learn to do this is critical. Faculty developers will gain insights into this volume on how to best support faculty learning.

Pamela L. Eddy
Editor

References

Bain, K. (2012). *What the best college students do*. Cambridge, MA: The Belknap Press of Harvard University.

Barber, J. P. (2012). Integration of learning: A grounded theory analysis of college students' learning. *American Educational Research Journal, 49*(3), 590–617. doi:10.3102/0002831212437854

Budwig, N. (2013). The learning sciences and liberal education. *Change: The Magazine of Higher Learning, 45*(3), 40–48.

Huber, G. (1991). Organizational learning: The contributing processes and the literatures. *Organization Science, 2*(2), 88–115.

Huber, M., & Hutchings, P. (2004). *Integrative learning: Mapping the terrain.* Washington, DC: The Association of American Colleges and Universities.

Kezar, A. J. (2005). What campuses need to know about organizational learning and the learning organization. In A. J. Kezar (Ed.), *New Directions for Higher Education: No. 131. Organizational learning in higher education* (pp. 7–22). San Francisco, CA: Jossey-Bass.

Kolb, D. A. (1998). Learning styles and disciplinary differences. In K. A. Feldman & M. B. Paulsen (Eds.), *Teaching and learning in the college classroom* (pp. 127–137). Needham Heights, MA: Simon & Schuster.

Mezirow, J. (1997). Transformative learning: Theory to practice. In P. Cranton (Ed.), *New Directions for Adult and Continuing Education: No. 74. Higher education: A global community* (pp. 5–12). San Francisco, CA: Jossey-Bass.

Pascarella, E. T., & Terenzini, P. T. (2005). *How college affects students: A third decade of research.* San Francisco, CA: Jossey-Bass.

PAMELA L. EDDY *is a professor of higher education at the College of William and Mary.*

1

Students integrate their learning experiences across contexts through a process of connecting, applying, and synthesizing information, knowledge, and skills.

Integration of Learning Model: How College Students Integrate Learning

James P. Barber

My interest in student learning, in particular the integration of learning (IOL), began well before I could name the concept. Prior to joining the faculty, I was a student affairs administrator, working directly with undergraduate programs and activities. In my work with students, much of my time was spent in individual advising meetings with student leaders. I often witnessed students integrating learning during these meetings. I have a vivid memory of a student leader who returned from a study abroad experience with an entirely new view of the world, which translated into how he prioritized his commitments and viewed his leadership position. Another student made clear connections between his finance major and the work he was doing as the treasurer of a student group. Time and time again, I saw students linking knowledge, skills, and information learned in different contexts.

As a doctoral student, I explored this type of integrated learning and found little empirical research on how college students go about integrating learning. My experiences, both personal and advising undergraduates, provided anecdotal evidence related to this type of learning, but limited educational research existed. Even with the growing literature on the need for students to integrate learning, how students actually put these pieces together is missing. This chapter explores the concept of undergraduate integration of learning, and positions it relative to various lenses for viewing learning across the institution (e.g., faculty learning, community engagement, and institutional or organizational learning).

This project was funded by the Center of Inquiry in the Liberal Arts at Wabash College. The author gratefully acknowledges the sponsorship of the Wabash National Study of Liberal Arts Education in support of this project.

NEW DIRECTIONS FOR HIGHER EDUCATION, no. 165, Spring 2014 © 2014 Wiley Periodicals, Inc.
Published online in Wiley Online Library (wileyonlinelibrary.com) • DOI: 10.1002/he.20079

Introduction to Integration of Learning

How do students "put things together"? Connecting disparate information and meaningfully synthesizing concepts have emerged as necessary skills for success in the knowledge economy of the 21st century. There have been an increasing number of calls in American society for college graduates to possess this ability to make connections among life experiences, academic studies, and their accumulated knowledge (American Association for Higher Education, American College Personnel Association, & National Association of Student Personnel Administrators, 1998; American College Personnel Association [ACPA], 1994; Association of American Colleges and Universities [AAC&U], 2002; AAC&U & Carnegie Foundation, 2004; National Association of Student Personnel Administrators and American College Personnel Association, 2004). This process is often termed "integration of learning."

I have developed the following definition of integration of learning, drawing from my own research and the various definitions discovered in a review of previous empirical studies:

> Integration of learning is the demonstrated ability to connect, apply, and/or synthesize information coherently from disparate contexts and perspectives, and make use of these new insights in multiple contexts. This includes the ability to connect the domain of ideas and philosophies to the everyday experience, from one field of study or discipline to another, from the past to the present, between campus and community life, from one part to the whole, from the abstract to the concrete, among multiple identity roles—and vice versa. (Barber, 2012, p. 593)

Recent research has identified experiences and curricula that may be prime contexts to foster integration, for example, first-year experience courses, undergraduate research, and writing intensive courses (see Wawrzynski and Baldwin's discussion of high-impact educational practices in Chapter 5 of this volume). However, despite an enthusiastic demand for integration of learning from both educators and employers, there is a lack of detailed information about the ways in which college students develop this skill, that is, the process or processes that students employ to learn in (and across) such rich contexts. Therefore, my work explores how integration of learning develops among traditional-aged college students.

I employ the self-authorship developmental model and the integration of learning construct as components of my theoretical framework. Self-authorship is a holistic model describing how individuals grow and change, often investigated in the context of higher education (Baxter Magolda, 1999, 2001; Kegan, 1994). Research demonstrates that there is a developmental trajectory toward self-authorship from a reliance on externally derived ways of thinking to more internally derived views (Baxter Magolda, 1999,

New Directions for Higher Education • DOI: 10.1002/he

2001; Kegan, 1994). This offers a perspective that informs inquiry into the development of integration of learning. Like self-authorship, integration of learning occurs via a similar developmental process (Barber, 2011).

As noted, integration of learning describes the process by which individuals bring together experience, knowledge, and skills across contexts. My research revealed three major categories of integration of learning: (a) *Connection*, the discovery of a similarity between ideas that themselves remain distinctive; (b) *Application*, the use of knowledge from one context in another; and (c) *Synthesis*, the creation of new knowledge by combining two or more insights (Barber, 2012). Next, I briefly review the methodology of my investigation of integration of learning.

Methods

The data for my analyses originated from the Wabash National Study of Liberal Arts Education (WNS). The WNS used a longitudinal concurrent mixed methods design in which two independent strands of data (surveys and interviews) were collected for addressing related but separate research questions; this chapter reports findings from the interview data (for an overview of the full study design, see http://www.liberalarts.wabash.edu/study-overview/). The longitudinal structure of the WNS allows a rare opportunity to examine an individual's development over time in detail. The WNS interview is semistructured in nature to allow students maximum freedom to identify relevant content yet enable interviewers to gain more depth into key topics using follow-up questions (Baxter Magolda & King, 2007, 2012). The main segments of the interview are constructed "in situ"—as the conversation unfolds, with a focus on the educational experiences students regard as key to their development and why these particular experiences are relevant. Interviewers seek to understand how students make meaning of these educational experiences (the interaction of their personal meaning making and the educational experience) to develop toward self-authorship.

I studied the interviews of students on two campuses, both of which are small, private, liberal arts institutions. The data from these two campuses are comprised of 272 longitudinal interviews ($n = 97$ individuals). Forty-five students from pseudonymous Hudson College (30 women and 15 men), and 52 students from Wabash College (all men) participated in interviews at the beginning of both their first and second years in college, resulting in 194 interviews. Forty-one of the Wabash men and 37 Hudson students (25 women and 12 men) returned for third-year interviews.

I used grounded theory to analyze the data and allow the *ways* in which students integrate learning (or fail to do so), and *how they make meaning* of that process, to emerge from the data rather than to establish a priori the elements of this developmental process. Data reduction began with what Strauss and Corbin (1998) call microanalysis, "the detailed line-by-line analysis necessary at the beginning of a study to generate initial categories (with their properties and dimensions) and to suggest relationships among categories" (p. 57). I later compared individuals' Year 1 interviews to their Year 2 and Year 3 (when available) interviews and then searched for emergent trends in development of integration of learning. A peer debriefer was involved with the analysis of both Year 1 and 2 data sets, to serve as a sounding board, offer a second perspective on the data, and bolster the trustworthiness of the study.

My research focuses on qualitative interview data from the WNS because in-depth constructivist interviews are effective in assessing the complex meaning making associated with self-authorship (Baxter Magolda & King, 2007) as well as the way(s) in which students integrate learning (Barber, 2011, 2012). In addition to the integration of learning analysis detailed above, each interview was assessed for self-authorship orientation independently (Baxter Magolda & King, 2012), but is not reported here.

Patterns in Student Integration of Learning

With assessments of both integration of learning and self-authorship for each interview, I was able to examine relationships and patterns between learning (i.e., integration of learning) and development (i.e., self-authorship). In categorizing the examples from the interviews, I found three main ways students integrated learning: establishing a connection, application across contexts, and synthesis of a new whole (Barber, 2012).

Defining Types of Integration.   The three ways in which students integrated learning have distinct characteristics. *Connection* is an experience where the student finds a common thread between concepts or experiences that still remain distinct. This type of integration may be fleeting, but is a clear acknowledgement that the student identifies similar elements, foundations, or characteristics. *Application* occurs when an idea or skill learned in one context is used in a different context. This stage is a more practical embodiment of integration than connection. In interviews with first-year students, application often appeared as the use of a high school skill or knowledge in college. *Synthesis* is a more complex and creative process, in which two or more ideas or skills are brought together to create a new whole; in this form of integration, students combine knowledge to enhance understanding and gain new insights (Barber, 2012).

I originally anticipated that a series of microsteps in integration of learning would be subtle increments that comprised the development of this skill. I called these increments "microsteps" to indicate the small strides that I envisioned carried young adults forward as they develop the capacity for integration of learning. However, the data from this sample of students did not indicate a sequential stage model for the microsteps of integration of learning; there was no evidence that college students first learned to connect, then to apply, then to synthesize, in that order. Rather, there was a developmental pattern that emerged from the data, albeit not the one I expected.

Adding a Developmental Lens.   Recall that each interview was assessed for developmental level, independently from the coding for integration of learning. When I analyzed the learning and development data together, I found that students with a less advanced developmental level, that is, more influenced by external frameworks (Baxter Magolda, 1999), favored one type of integration, usually connection or application. Students who were more advanced in terms of self-authorship, or moving toward an internal foundation (Baxter Magolda, 1999), tended to use all three methods of integration more equally. However, each of the participants used all three ways of integrating learning to some extent.

These data support a developmental pattern within integration of learning categories, but the ordering of the three IOL stages was not necessarily linear. Findings from my study suggest that students with more advanced self-authorship levels use more intricate varieties of integration of learning, such as synthesis, and integrate learning more often than their peers with more externally derived ways of seeing the world, who trend toward simpler integration such as concrete application.

The data analyzed in this study support the notion of integration of learning as a constructive-developmental process rather than a lock-step stage model. There is a clear developmental sequence in how integration of learning capacity advances among the college students in this sample, which is undergirded by the progression of self-authorship from external frameworks to internal foundations for understanding. The microsteps of integration of learning that I uncovered are not rigidly sequential per se, but I posit that there is a development of greater complexity that occurs *among* the microsteps, as well as *within* each microstep or category, based on students' developmental levels and ways of meaning making. The nuance of the way students integrate their learning depends on the student's individual development.

Based on my insights from the data, I argue that there is an increasing level of complexity from connection, to application, to synthesis, but do not find that mastering one type of integration before learning to use a more complex form is necessary. Instead, students use all three forms of integration of learning in an increasingly cohesive way as the individual advances developmentally. Students who are less advanced in terms of self-authorship integrate less and rely more on the "hands-on" approach of the application category. As a student's developmental level (as measured by self-authorship) increases, the frequency of integration also increases, and students use connection, application, and synthesis more equally. In this light, I represent the development of integration of learning for undergraduates more like a kaleidoscope than a stairway. Figure 1.1 illustrates how

Figure 1.1. Integration of Learning Categories

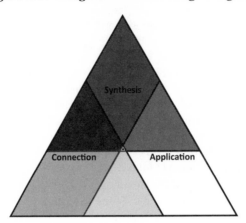

students use all three forms of integration of learning in an increasingly complex way as the individual advances developmentally, as opposed to a stage-model approach.

Next, I discuss some of the important challenges students face in terms of integrating their own learning.

Considerations for Undergraduate Learning

Three of the key issues facing students in regard to learning are (a) compartmentalization, (b) the ever-increasing collection of digital tools available, and (c) a lack of opportunities for reflection. Even as students have numerous digital tools that serve to advance integration, such as social media platforms, ubiquitous access to the Internet via laptops and smart phones, and the resulting access to vast amounts of information and resources online, the culture of American higher education often trends toward compartmentalization. Courses are often viewed as stand-alone modules, limited to the four walls of the classroom and without connection to students' prior experiences or knowledge. Courses with prerequisites sometimes draw on knowledge and skills from previous classroom experiences, but rarely are students encouraged to link classroom learning to their experiences outside of the classroom in jobs and internships, relationships, student organizations, or athletic teams. Faculty members should be intentional and explicit about opening the door to broader integration for students and inviting students' learning from other contexts into the classroom because research has shown the benefits of building on prior knowledge for learners (e.g., Baxter Magolda & King, 2004; Holt-Reynolds, 1992; Thompson & Zamboanga, 2003).

The technology available to students, faculty, and institutions is a double-edged sword. As the number of digital tools grows, wireless Internet access becomes increasingly available, and mobile devices permit a constant connection to both other people and information, the potential for integration of learning also grows. However, these same tools can serve to bolster compartmentalization. Some platforms (e.g., Blackboard, Moodle) are viewed as academically related spaces to interact with course content and faculty members, while others (e.g., Facebook, Twitter) are socially oriented spaces to interact with friends, family members, and popular culture. There is great potential to cross boundaries in learning with these technologies if the major stakeholders come together to find ways to use them productively to advance learning. Personally, I have had success with experimenting with integrating Twitter into my teaching and see exciting opportunities to capitalize on new media and emerging technologies to break down contextual barriers rather than strengthen them.

Students also need more opportunities to reflect on their own learning. Many students interviewed for the Wabash National Study of Liberal Arts Education shared that they enjoyed the annual interview because it provided a space to reflect on their experiences and talk about their learning. There did not appear to be other intentional opportunities for reflection in their daily lives or academic programs (at least that students discussed in the interviews). Students often integrated learning "in the moment" during the interviews and related that the conversation served as a venue for reflection and making connections between learning across contexts. In this light, I see the interview itself as an intervention that has potential for promoting student learning and development, one that could be easily recreated via intentional, regular (even annual) conversations with faculty or staff members. Academic advising is one venue where this interaction already happens; senior capstone experiences or portfolios may be another productive experience to tap for promoting integration intentionally. Residence life programs are also uniquely positioned to foster conversations with faculty or staff for students who live on campus.

Integration of Learning Within and Among Stakeholders. I posit that undergraduate students integrate learning by connecting, applying, and synthesizing. Yet, my research has found that there is a lack of mentors or guides involved in students' integration. Although students are clearly integrating learning across contexts, and doing so more frequently as they grow and advance during the undergraduate years, there are few instances in the interview data that show involvement or influence of faculty members or educational administrators in this process. More often, students are turning to peers for support and guidance in connecting their learning. However, based on the student interviews, students are interested in this type of conversation with campus staff and faculty members.

Based on the increasing frequency and urgency of calls for more efforts to promote integration of learning as a collegiate outcome, I anticipated very little integration would be present in college students' experiences today. However, I found just the opposite. Students are integrating learning in a number of different ways (connection, application, synthesis, and combinations of these methods) in a wide variety of contexts. For example, Mack, in his second year at Wabash College, described how he made meaning of the institution's *Gentleman's Rule*, the institution's single rule of conduct, which states: "The student is expected to conduct himself at all times, both on and off campus, as a gentleman and a responsible citizen" (Wabash College, 2013, para. 3). Mack reflected:

> That's more or less expounding on the ideals and morals that I've learned not only going to church when I was younger, in scouts with the Scout Law, twelve points that a Scout is all these things and this is how you lead your life. So I mean it's part of my code and moral compass that I've adapted into all of the things that I've learned so far. This is the right thing to do. This is how you need to act as a person.

Mack brings together his prior experience and the text of the Gentleman's Rule to create his current understanding of the rule. He synthesizes the concepts and ideals from his church and the Boy Scout Law, along with the words of the Wabash Gentleman's Rule, to form his understanding of what the rule means and how to enact it in his life. Mack makes uncoerced links between the moral aspects of Christianity, Scouting, and the Gentleman's Rule, synthesizing his concept of the Gentleman's Rule from elements of each.

Integration of learning among college students is not limited to the classroom or institutional context, and in fact the integration that is going on outside the classroom enhances the classroom learning and vice versa. Quinn, in his third year at Hudson College, described his synthesizing learning experience as follows:

> When I came here [to Hudson College], I didn't know what I wanted to do. I didn't have a drive. I had some drive, but it's very different than what I have now, and I don't think I valued my own self-worth as much. I think from the professors, from the classes, from the people I met here, from the experiences I've taken off, from the readings, from the in-class participation, from living with these people, from the administrators on campus, from all these experiences I've gained the sense that consequences in life are important, and I have discovered these new pathways of thinking and new concepts and new ideas and new fields that will let me branch out and just be able to participate and engage and affect and understand and comprehend and work through these issues that better the world.

Quinn synthesized concepts from numerous sources, including authorities, trusted peers, coursework, and out-of-class activities. He draws upon these multiple sources to create his own belief about the importance of consequence. In this example, Quinn synthesized these disparate elements and then applied this newly synthesized perspective to real-world decisions about his own actions and the consequences that accompany them. As educators, practitioners, and researchers, we are only seeing a partial picture if we focus on "classroom integration" in isolation (Barber, 2011).

Despite the wealth of integration that is occurring among students, higher education literature focuses on the need for more integration, painting student experiences as largely disconnected and isolated. My research found that integration of learning is alive and well on college campuses, but that faculty and staff are frequently not involved in or aware of the connections students are making. More educator involvement is an area that I argue is in need of attention and intentional intervention. Students in the study responded quite favorably to their conversations with interviewers, and some students integrated learning "in the moment" as a byproduct of the interviews. In the next section, I discuss how my findings about undergraduate integration of learning can inform practice and policy at the faculty and institutional levels.

Implications: Transferable Approaches to Integrating Learning. Taking a broad view of learning is an approach that will aid the various stakeholder groups (i.e., students, faculty, institutional, and community leaders) to progress toward a more seamless and inclusive learning environment. No one stakeholder group has a monopoly on learning. My research found that learning is happening all the time and in a variety of contexts in and out of the classroom, on and off campus, and virtual and in person. As expressed earlier, for many students, learning is compartmentalized by context; each context is a silo with independent content, relationships, expectations, and culture. You might envision this as separate silos for academics, work, home, student activities, and so forth. And, there are still more silos or divisions within each of these contexts. For example, in the academic area, each discipline (or even each course within a discipline) is a silo with its own content, culture, and so forth. As a result, students may not perceive knowledge from general education requirements as relevant to courses in their majors.

Decompartmentalizing involves identifying expectations for teaching and learning and establishing student learning outcomes that are consistent across contexts. David Leslie refers to these as *orthogonal* outcomes, to illustrate that they cut across disciplines, with the outcomes perpendicular to the disciplinary silos (see Chapter 4 of this volume). These are the outcomes that should be common to all undergraduates. Although deconstructing these silo barriers may be completely unrealistic, we as scholars, teachers, and educational leaders can work to make the boundaries within our spheres of influence more permeable and allow for a greater degree of integration.

My research on undergraduate integration of learning has clear implications for practice on college campuses. Currently, I am focusing on how
best to operationalize what I have learned about integration of learning into
best practices for college experiences, broadly, in academic affairs, student
affairs, and the world beyond our campuses. This work seeks to shift what
I have learned about *how* students integrate learning (i.e., connecting, applying, and synthesizing) to inform *what* experiences promote integration
of learning across contexts. For example, the LEAP Vision for Learning
(AAC&U, 2011) outlines a set of learning outcomes that may be enhanced
by attention to the stages of integration of learning (Barber, 2012). Bridging
various learning domains together intentionally creates opportunities for
integration.

Constructing an Inclusive Learning Theory

In order to create a larger theory of learning that would be applicable across
boundaries of the traditional silos in higher education, we need to bring
together scholars who study learning in various contexts and convene conversations. This volume begins such a conversation. Beyond simply getting people together, we need to work on establishing a common language.
Even within the student learning subfield, there is little agreement on the
terminology of learning, as evidenced by references to integration of learning, integrated learning, connected learning, experiential learning, engaged
learning, and so forth. Most of these terms are used interchangeably in day-
to-day conversations, although they may have very nuanced differences in
the research literature.

A larger theory of learning must draw from the robust literature on
adult learning. Too often, college learning and development theory focuses
on the "traditional-aged" college student, 18–24-year-olds and attending a
four-year institution full time. Demographic data reveal that most undergraduate students enrolled today do not fit this "traditional" description
(NCES, 2012). College educators must investigate the adult learning literature and embrace the concept of andragogy as a viable alternative to, or
perhaps a complement to, conventional notions of pedagogy.

Lastly, in order to create a larger theory of learning that might have multiple applications, it will be necessary to eliminate some of the institutional
and organizational barriers to integration of learning. We need to identify
orthogonal outcomes, the ones that cut across contexts, and use these student learning outcomes as avenues for collaborating across campus, as well
as beyond our institutions.

References

American Association for Higher Education, American College Personnel Association, & National Association of Student Personnel Administrators. (1998).

Powerful partnerships: A shared responsibility for learning. Retrieved from http://www.myacpa.org/powerful-partnerships-shared-responsibility-learning

American College Personnel Association (ACPA). (1994). *The student learning imperative.* Washington, DC: Author.

Association of American Colleges and Universities (AAC&U). (2002). *Greater expectations: A new vision for learning as a nation goes to college.* Retrieved from http://www.greaterexpectations.org/

Association of American Colleges and Universities (AAC&U). (2011). *The LEAP vision for learning: Outcomes, practices, impact, and employers' views.* Retrieved from http://www.aacu.org/leap/documents/leap_vision_summary.pdf

Association of American Colleges and Universities (AAC&U) & Carnegie Foundation. (2004). *A statement on integrative learning.* Washington, DC: Author.

Barber, J. P. (2011, March). *Mapping relationships between integration of learning and student development: Examining a third year of data.* Paper presented at the NASPA Annual Conference, Philadelphia, PA.

Barber, J. P. (2012). Integration of learning: A grounded theory analysis of college students' learning. *American Educational Research Journal, 49*(3), 590–617. doi:10.3102/0002831212437854

Baxter Magolda, M. B. (1999). *Creating contexts for learning and self-authorship: Constructive-developmental pedagogy.* Nashville, TN: Vanderbilt University Press.

Baxter Magolda, M. B. (2001). *Making their own way: Narratives for transforming higher education to promote self-development.* Sterling, VA: Stylus.

Baxter Magolda, M. B., & King, P. M. (2004). *Learning partnerships: Theory and models of practice to educate for self-authorship.* Sterling, VA: Stylus.

Baxter Magolda, M. B., & King, P. M. (2007). Constructing conversations to assess meaning-making: Self-authorship interviews. *Journal of College Student Development, 48*(5), 491–508. doi:10.1353/csd.2007.0055

Baxter Magolda, M. B., & King, P. M. (2012). Assessing meaning making and self-authorship: Theory, research, and application. *ASHE Higher Education Report Series, 38*(3), 1–138. doi:10.1002/aehe.20003

Holt-Reynolds, D. (1992). Personal history-based beliefs as relevant prior knowledge in course work. *American Educational Research Journal, 29*(2), 325–349. doi:10.3102/00028312029002325

Kegan, R. (1994). *In over our heads: The mental demands of modern life.* Cambridge, MA: Harvard University Press.

National Association of Student Personnel Administrators and American College Personnel Association. (2004). *Learning reconsidered: A campus-wide focus on the student experience.* Washington, DC: Author.

National Center for Education Statistics (NCES). (2012). *Digest of Education Statistics, 2011* (NCES 2012-001). Retrieved from http://nces.ed.gov/programs/digest/d11/ch_3.asp

Strauss, A., & Corbin, J. (1998). *Basics of qualitative research: Techniques and procedures for developing grounded theory.* Thousand Oaks, CA: Sage.

Thompson, R. A., & Zamboanga, B. L. (2003). Prior knowledge and its relevance to student achievement in introduction to psychology. *Teaching of Psychology, 30*(2), 96–101. doi:10.1207/S15328023TOP3002_02

Wabash College. (2013). *Trust an 18 year old?* Retrieved from http://www.wabash.edu/eod/trust/

James P. Barber is an assistant professor of higher education at the College of William and Mary.

2

As adult learners, faculty members approach new experiences based on events of the past, but this underlying framework of understanding is challenged when they work abroad for an extended period of time.

Faculty as Border Crossers: A Study of Fulbright Faculty

Pamela L. Eddy

Internationalization efforts on college campuses are on the increase. An expectation and goal of a university education is to develop global competencies of college graduates (Knight, 2009). Involvement in international endeavors also helps to heighten institutional prestige through higher global rankings (Hazelkorn, 2011), which are based in part on faculty research productivity and international reputation. Today's faculty lead study abroad classes, conduct internationally based research, and incorporate international perspectives in their teaching. Fulbright awards provide one venue in which faculty are able to immerse themselves into an international context, develop their teaching and research, and create and maintain connections for partnerships. The research presented in this chapter was conducted in Ireland with both U.S. and Irish Fulbright scholars. A qualitative study using a phenomenology design included 10 scholars, four were Irish scholars who had Fulbright awards in the United States and six were U.S. scholars with Fulbright awards in Ireland. The questions guiding the study sought to understand faculty learning in an international context.

In 2003, Ireland's higher education policy was reviewed by the Education Committee of the Organisation for Economic Co-operation and Development (OECD), of which Ireland is one of the 20 member countries (OECD, 2006). One of the outcomes of this report was a need to increase recruitment of international students. Not only is there a financial benefit to recruiting a diverse student body, the creation of a diverse student culture enhances learning for all students and helps fulfill the civic and educational mission of universities (Hurtado, 2007). Many colleges and

The author gratefully acknowledges funding from the Irish Fulbright Program in support of this project.

NEW DIRECTIONS FOR HIGHER EDUCATION, no. 165, Spring 2014 © 2014 Wiley Periodicals, Inc.
Published online in Wiley Online Library (wileyonlinelibrary.com) • DOI: 10.1002/he.20080

universities in the United States are also focused on including global competency as a goal for student learning outcomes upon graduation (Romano, 2002). Study abroad programs have long been a staple of the college experience for students, but the need to compete in a global economy presses institutions to think more intentionally about how to internationalize curriculum, educate students to become global citizens, and engage with institutions around the world in joint degree programs and cooperative research. A linchpin to these efforts is college faculty members.

Altbach and Lewis (1996) reported findings from the 1992 Carnegie Foundation for the Advancement of Teaching's International Survey and noted that only one in three U.S. faculty had taken at least one trip abroad for study or research. Recently, a team of researchers conducted a survey to determine what changes have occurred for U.S. faculty in the past decade. Finkelstein, Walker, and Chen (2013) found that faculty members are still insular in their scholarship and in internationalizing the curriculum. The researchers note that adult years spent abroad were the most pervasive and powerful predictor of faculty internationalizing their curriculum, working with and publishing in collaboration with international colleagues, having research that is international in scope, and publishing in foreign countries. Pointedly, the American Council on Education's (2012) *Mapping Internationalization on U.S. Campuses* survey, conducted in 2011, indicated decreases in faculty development support to assist internationalization efforts and corresponding decreases in internationally focused curriculum. Calls for creating comprehensive internationalization still show mixed success (Peterson & Helms, 2013).

Though insufficient, there is still support for faculty efforts to create comprehensive internationalization. For example, Beloit College created a program to allow its faculty opportunities abroad to help foster faculty learning that could be translated into curricular changes to improve student global competencies (Brewer, 2010). Efforts at the College of William and Mary also illustrate changes underway to help with internationalization efforts (Eddy, Barber, Holly, Brush, & Bohan, 2013). For faculty members without these types of institutional supports, however, efforts are often individually driven.

U.S. Senator J. William Fulbright introduced a bill that was established as a law in 1946 creating the Fulbright Program. The intention of the program is to help build bridges between countries that create an enhanced understanding of and compassion for world affairs and provide the basis for peaceful coexistence. In Ireland, the Fulbright Program was started in 1957 to provide scholarships to Irish citizens to lecture, research, or study in the United States and for U.S. citizens to lecture, research, or study in Ireland (Fulbright, 2013). The Fulbright Program provides a forum ripe for investigating the faculty experience in an international setting and determining how faculty perceive the experience affects or will affect their teaching and research upon their return to their home country.

Literature Review

The increased demand for college graduates to possess intercultural skills and competencies (American Council on Education [ACE], 2012) requires internationalization on campus that includes these same skills in faculty members. One way that "faculty gain international perspectives is through teaching and research opportunities abroad and by building relationships with peers in other countries" (ACE, 2012, p. 14). Yet only 8% of institutional promotion and tenure guidelines specifically recognize this type of international work when considering tenure or promotion. Moreover, funding to support faculty travel abroad has declined nationally (ACE, 2012) and fiscal exigency in Ireland has reduced university funding (Higher Education Authority, 2013). Thus, while there is recognition of the need to increase internationalization efforts on campus, there is a lack of structural support and recognition for the efforts of faculty in their international work (Eddy et al., 2013). As well, a gap exists in the literature in understanding how faculty who do pursue international experiences incorporate their learning experiences into internationalization efforts on their home campuses.

To understand better the process of learning for the faculty involved in international experiences, it is important to look at adult learning theory. When faculty members work abroad, they incorporate their new experiences into their underlying schemas and ways of knowing. Andragogy (Knowles, 1970) describes the ways in which adults learn. The five basic features of andragogy include that adults: (a) have rich life experiences to link to new learning, (b) employ self-directed learning, (c) are goal oriented and practical, (d) are intrinsically motivated, and (e) learn based on their life role needs. As adult learners, faculty and campus leaders continuously sift through new information and experiences to determine how it meshes with what is known, what is new, and what should be incorporated for future understanding. Thus, while working abroad, faculty members understand their new encounters through a filter of past experiences.

According to Kegan and Lahey (2009), there are three plateaus for adult mental development: the socialized mind, the self-authoring mind, and the self-transforming mind. The attributes of the socialized phase of development focus on being a team player, aligning with the group, and seeking direction. The self-authoring phase instead finds individuals driven by their own agendas, problem solving, and becoming independent. Finally, the self-transforming mind phase finds individuals valuing multiple perspectives, modifying plans based on feedback, and relying on interdependency with others. A feature of this model of development is the lengthening of time between development phases and time at each plateau phase; ultimately, fewer and fewer people achieve the higher levels of development.

The conceptual model for this study utilized adult learning theory (Knowles, 1980; Merriam & Brockett, 2007). Kegan and Lahey's (2009) plateaus for adult learning helped inform the location used by faculty members to "hook" their new learning to existing approaches to learning. Literature on the changing nature of faculty work (Gappa, Austin, & Trice, 2007) and the support of international faculty development (ACE, 2012) also informed this research as the demands on faculty time influence the type and extent of learning that occurs for faculty members.

Methods

This research used qualitative methods to investigate a particular phenomenon (Creswell, 2007), which in this research was the teaching and learning experiences of faculty members participating in an exchange program. The research questions underpinning this study were: How do faculty members describe their own learning in an international context? How do faculty members describe teaching and learning in their new context? How do faculty members anticipate their international experience will change their own teaching?

A qualitative method of data collection was used for this research, hermeneutic phenomenology (Van Manen, 1990), as this allowed for delving into the topic using the participants' voices and perspectives (Creswell, 2007). Phenomenology provided a focus on the experiences of our participants as faculty members teaching in a new context, whereas using hermeneutics allowed for interpretation of the phenomena versus merely describing it. The goal was to understand how faculty members incorporated the experience of teaching and researching abroad into their own learning. The focus in particular centered on the components of the international experience that altered individual thinking about teaching and learning and what it means for creating an environment that fosters intercultural competency for students.

Participants were purposefully selected. Polkinghorne (1989) argues that between five and 25 participants should be included when conducting a phenomenology. A total of 30 U.S. scholars were awarded Fulbright scholarships for an exchange in Ireland in the 2008–2009 academic year. Of this total, 12 were engaged in teaching responsibilities. All were contacted for participation in this research and six participated in the study. A total of nine Irish scholars who taught in another country within the past five years were also contacted for inclusion in this research and four ultimately participated. A semistructured interview protocol allowed for the investigation of the phenomenon of the learning experience. Interviews occurred face-to-face in Ireland in spring 2009.

The participants represented a narrow range of ethnic groups (all White) and were predominately men (only one woman was included in the study). Quotes appearing in this chapter are coded to represent gender (women = F; men = M) and country of origin (US = United States; IRE = Ireland). The demographic portrait of the participants is common in Ireland, with the majority of the population composed of Whites. The gender participation in Fulbright Scholar programs in the years under review was predominately men (seven of the nine Irish scholars and 10 of the 12 U.S. scholars). Participants worked in a variety of Irish and American universities, ranging from private liberal arts colleges to public research universities. Each was embedded in a smaller department and most of their reflections dealt with work at the departmental level versus the university. The Irish scholars and the U.S. scholars ranged in their time in their host country, with visits ranging from a full year to others that were six months or a semester in length.

A limitation of this research is the focus on two countries for the exchanges, Ireland and the United States. Cultural context of other countries may have different types of learning occurring for the faculty members. In particular, when language and customs are markedly different, other levels of cognitive dissonance might occur. As well, my own identity construction and participation in the Fulbright Scholar program may create bias. To guard against this bias, I used member checking and a peer reviewer. Geertz (1993) argued that researchers and participants are equally involved in creating understanding of the findings. Thus, my positionality as cultural insider not only provided an ability to establish rapport with the participants (Ganga & Scott, 2006) but also meant I had to guard against making assumptions about participants' meaning. Specifically, I was a U.S. scholar doing research in Ireland, though I did not have any teaching responsibilities to allow for comparisons of the classroom examples participants related. Because I brought emic perspectives to the research, I was particularly careful to bracket my assumptions during data analysis (Creswell, 2007).

Findings and Discussion

Three findings emerged from the data. First, disequilibrium provided a launch point for learning. When pushed out of their comfort zones, faculty members were open to new learning. Second, faculty experienced a move from expert/insider to novice/outsider as a result of the new international context. Old and engrained understandings were tested in the new environment. Finally, an integration of personal and professional reflection occurred that resulted in learning crossing the boundaries of work and family, and home and host country. Ultimately, transformational learning occurred due to critical reflection by faculty members of their experiences. Implications for practice include bridging the faculty experience abroad with opportunities to enhance student learning, providing faculty development opportunities in advance of faculty leaving the country to allow for enhanced learning, and building theory regarding the integration of learning for faculty members.

For the U.S. scholars, Irish ancestry or love of Irish literature and music were motivators in seeking out Ireland as the site for their Fulbright. When asked *Why Ireland?*, the responses included: "My family background—this is where we're from and I wanted to come back and stay here an extended amount of time" (F-US); "I'm an Irishman!" (M-US); "I toured Ireland and met people who had read all my books—and I was famous! . . . I found a network I accidentally had fallen into" (M-US). For the Irish scholars, studying in the United States provided an opportunity to work with high-level researchers and to connect their work using an interdisciplinary perspective. One of the Irish scholars commented, "I find that in my work [in Ireland], I'm asked, What are you? Are you this or that? Where in America, people were very interested in this kind of work and openness. That was very refreshing" (M-IRE). The Irish scholars had connections to U.S. researchers based on their disciplinary associations and built on this social network to secure their institutional affiliations in the United States. Despite this sense of belonging and fit, challenges emerged for the faculty working abroad.

Disequilibrium.   Faculty members faced a number of incidents in which they were pushed out of their typical patterns of understanding. One faculty member commented, "I haven't been alone probably ever in my life, ever [laughs]. I went from sharing rooms with brothers to roommates in college to marriage. Being alone and independent was a new experience. I think I've grown in ways I probably don't deserve" (M-US). This faculty member recognized how the disequilibrium created as result of his moving halfway around the world provided a context for him to grow and develop. This type of self-authorship was not evident to this faculty before. Because many of the Fulbright scholars traveled with family members, the learning they experienced bridged the professional and the personal and involved the assimilation of family members into the new locale as well.

Likewise, other faculty described how they initially felt isolated, as one physics faculty noted, "It turned out professionally that it was hard to get started" (M-US). Getting used to the shared values of the educational structure in the host country was an adjustment. One U.S. faculty commented, "I was really surprised how international students were. I guess I wasn't expecting that. I had this image I would come in and I would be teaching Irish students . . . and it's been really interesting to see these international students coming in brand new to Ireland too and blind to the culture" (F-US).

An American faculty noted that the course structure was different and contained more of a hands-on component. Another found that the fact that most students didn't attend lectures and only showed up for the exams to be disconcerting. Whereas another offered, "The system is set up [in my department] at the University College-Dublin so that it's impossible to teach the way Americans consider teaching a college class" (M-US). He added, "I was not given any orientation—they took for granted that I was immediately oriented to a system that was absolutely alien." Irish faculty members also referenced differences they experienced in the classroom.

According to one Irish faculty, American students sought more structure for classroom teaching and desired their hard work to equate to a good grade. The Irish faculty noted, "The students would think 'I worked hard enough so I deserve it [a good grade].' I found that difficult to deal with." In this case, the disequilibrium was based on differences in classroom expectations of faculty and students. This same faculty noted, "My role as a professor here is to give information...whether they get it or not doesn't really affect me and does not matter."

One Irish faculty described his culture shock in the classroom. He added, "I was really not prepared for it to be quite honest on a whole range." His placement at an elite U.S. university exposed him to students who were "the brightest students in their city," and as a result in classroom participation the students felt "that every word that they say they think has to be pure gold. So there is absolutely no free speech for random ideas is another thing." The type of student participation and expectations in class created a different teaching context for the exchange faculty. The different expectations of faculty work were a source of initial disequilibrium and ultimate learning. Participants clearly identified experiences that located them in the self-authoring developmental stage (Kegan & Lahey, 2009). They were self-directed and innovative, but also identified traits in the transforming stage of development. The faculty members noted how they changed plans based on student and colleague feedback and how they now understood more fully multiple perspectives of teaching and learning and their faculty role.

Expert to Novice.   As adult learners, the faculty in this study came to their new experiences with a vast range of backgrounds and expertise. Yet, the move across the ocean to work in another institution left them ungrounded by their sense of disequilibrium and by the fact that they were now novices as they approached their new positions. One U.S. faculty recounted his first weeks at his Irish college, "I was really nervous those first few weeks because they started to assign me modules [to teach] and I didn't want to do that. Partly because I hadn't taught that module before, even though it was related to the research I do, and teaching a new module for me is very intensive" (M-US). By the spring term, this faculty member noted, "I felt like I had more expertise." Moving back to a novice position resulted in learning opportunities for the faculty members in their host countries, with all the faculty noting how they had grown over the course of their stay. Faculty began entering the self-transforming stage (Kegan & Lahey, 2009) as they gained multiple perspectives on their teaching.

The difference in the teaching structure also meant that final exams in Ireland were prepared three months ahead of time and reviewed by external examiners. This procedure was foreign to the U.S. faculty. As well, the courses were shorter and students often did not attend lectures. One U.S. faculty noted, "One thing that was very difficult for me was to try to compress my normal teaching into a shorter timeframe. I had to do a lot of thinking about what to present to the students" (F-US). This self-reflection resulted in questioning of the assumptions about how to format the time with students and to trust that the students were engaged with the reading materials outside of class to provide discussion of advanced topics when in class together.

For an American film instructor, the adjustment was difficult given the lack of space and format to show films for discussion. He noted, "In America, I'd show 20–25 films per class and I'm teaching two classes, so I tried to bring 80 films. They didn't have a film room, so they bought a DVD player and put us in a room with a big screen." The difference in physical space and expectations about technology pressed faculty to approach their teaching differently. An American music faculty related how for each of his classes he had to cart equipment to the lecture classroom.

The extreme of a move from expert to novice occurred for a faculty member charged with teaching a lecture on the civil war—a content area far removed from his discipline. He reflected, "It ruined my whole semester. Thinking about it. It was the low point of my existence" (M-US).

A shift for one of the Irish faculty involved the range of experience of students in his U.S. class and the level of engagement. He commented on his lecture preparation offering, "I guess what was interesting was how useless this was in several of the seminars, because I would put up the first slide and the discussion would start and I'd realize that I had 30–40 slides and I never got past one." Heightened levels of class participation resulted in a shift in his teaching style relative to what worked for him in Ireland versus what he faced in a U.S. classroom. When asked about his experiences teaching in the United States, another Irish faculty kept commenting, "So, this was completely new," and offered how some of the strategies he learned during his U.S. Fulbright he brought back to his teaching in Ireland.

One of the Irish faculty attended conferences in Montana and Oregon and observed how these experiences challenged what he understood as the norm for U.S. higher education. He commented on the poverty he saw in some of the rural locales, but how the conference participants were eager to learn about Irish history and the peace movement in Northern Ireland. This faculty member worked to reconcile this dissonance in his experiences. Again, the growth for the faculty in general occurred due to their firsthand experience in understanding the different perspectives of teaching, student approaches to learning, and assumptions of classroom practices.

Transformation via Integration.   The faculty in this study all noted how their experiences had transformed their way of thinking, highlighting the third phase of Kegan and Lahey's (2009) stage model of self-transformation. But, this transformation was not based only on their professional work during their Fulbright. As noted above, the purpose of the Fulbright is to understand more about another culture. Faculty members integrated the learning they were doing through their work and lived experiences in the community, reflecting on previously held assumptions that ultimately resulted in exhibiting attributes of the self-transforming mind. For the bulk of the faculty, their Fulbright was the longest period of their adult life in which they lived in a different culture. Though some had experienced study abroad, this new experience as an adult was different. As one U.S. faculty commented, "And it turned out, for me trying something different on sabbatical, having a different experience from what I was used to, going out of my comfort zone, intrigued me, even though it makes more work." Exposure to different teaching strategies, new university processes, and being in a different environment required the faculty to question underlying assumptions held by their previous experiences and to rely on others in the host institution for information and feedback. Faculty participants were able to articulate specific takeaways they learned in their experience. As one faculty reflected, "I've been able to compare and contrast with what I'm used to" (M-US).

As one U.S. Fulbrighter noted, "I found, just by asking someone their name, and when you see them again, going to a place regularly, that person remembers you and suddenly it feels like, 'Oh I have a friend here.' Back home there are faces I see every day, in a coffee shop or something, and I've never even thought about asking them what their name was." Also, having an international experience highlighted for faculty that the problems faced in their discipline are not unique to their home country, but truly are global in nature.

The Fulbright provided the faculty with an opportunity to think about their home country differently, too. One U.S. faculty noted how he appreciated the United States differently as a result of the experience, but also how it made him realize what he formerly took for granted as a professor regarding the autonomy in the U.S. system of higher education. An Irish faculty reflected that in America his focus on interdisciplinary work was valued, whereas in Ireland he often faced questions that attempted to locate his work in one discipline or another. This faculty found he faced a kind of "status shock" when returning to Ireland. He expanded on how this status shock differed from culture shock: "You know from the openness of America—to giving a number of keynote address to coming back where you are just a regular PhD person." He found the transformational experience he had in the United States difficult to maintain upon his return home due to teaching structures in place and disciplinary norms. He maintained ties with his host U.S. institution that allowed him an outlet that valued the work he was doing.

The Irish faculty had all been in other countries prior to their Fulbright given the proximity of Ireland to the European continent. Thus, their views on the international experience were grounded most often in the local university and classroom culture versus in the experience of visiting or living somewhere outside their home country. Yet, the culture of the United States differed enough from their European experience that their day-to-day living still had some influence on the creation of a more complex understanding of differences.

Conclusion

For the Fulbright faculty in this study, crossing borders provided them with an opportunity to question their assumptions about teaching, to explore a culture different than their own, and to grow both personally and professionally in ways they had not anticipated. The disequilibrium of time spent abroad and the shift from expert to novice provided a context ripe for learning. Although faculty had responsibilities in their temporary positions, they had freedom to explore new topics and areas given their release from their home institution responsibilities. The time away provided a space for reflection and put in stark relief assumptions they formerly held. These faculty members represent the small percentage that Kegan and Lahey (2009) found in their last phase of adult learning—self-transforming. Yet, even though the faculty participants observed how they had changed, it is important to note that transformation occurred along a continuum depending on life stage, experiences, and level of reflection.

This research holds a number of implications for practice. First, the experiences of the faculty participants underscore what Finkelstein et al. (2013) concluded, namely, how critical it is to get faculty to visit other countries. This conclusion is particularly salient for U.S. faculty who travel abroad less frequently compared to their European counterparts who may enter another country in sometimes as little as one or two hours of travel. But, gains were also evident for the Irish faculty as so much of the borrowing of higher education system models around the world builds on what is done in the United States. Second, the faculty all noted how their learning and questioning of previous assumptions would transform their own teaching practices upon return to their home institutions. Thus, students at the home institutions will benefit from the faculty learning as these teachers transform and internationalize their own teaching. A direct influence of the Fulbright faculty on students at their host institution also occurred. As one Irish faculty member related, "I continue to write reference letters for [the students at my host institution]." Finally, the transformational learning that occurred for the faculty members resulted from the ways they integrated what they were learning across professional and personal domains. Much as Barber (2012) advocates for student integration of learning, the same need for integration holds true for faculty learning too. Faculty learning how to navigate in a foreign land, living among different communities, and working in new contexts all stretched former understandings. Having a space in which to reflect on their new learning and sharing it with others helped reify the transformation. Having expectations challenged helped in achieving new learning and perspectives.

Not all universities or colleges provide the opportunity for sabbatical leaves and the limited number of Fulbright awards results in only a select few having an opportunity to partake in these types of exchanges. However, faculty members and institutions can support this type of transformational learning in a number of ways. Brewer (2010) showcases how a small liberal arts campus helped support faculty learning with short international trips. The opportunity to host visiting scholars on campus provides another chance for learning about different systems and approaches. Finally, technology opens the world in very different ways so that exchanges can occur virtually. What this research concludes is that faculty learning is enhanced by a change in context that disrupts typical patterns of behaviors. Through instances of disequilibrium and vulnerability of moving from expert to novice, transformational learning is possible.

References

Altbach, P. G., & Lewis, L. S. (1996). The academic profession in international perspective. In P. G. Altbach (Ed.), *The international academic profession portraits of fourteen countries* (pp. 3–48). Princeton, NJ: Carnegie Foundation for the Advancement of Teaching.

American Council on Education (ACE). (2012). *Mapping internationalization on U.S. campuses: 2012 edition*. Washington, DC: Author.

Barber, J. P. (2012). Integration of learning: A grounded theory analysis of college students' learning. *American Educational Research Journal, 49*(3), 590–617. doi:10.3102/0002831212437854

Brewer, E. (2010). Leveraging partnerships to internationalize the liberal arts college: Campus internationalization and the faculty. In P. L. Eddy (Ed.), *New Directions for Higher Education: No. 150. International collaborations: Opportunities, strategies, challenges* (pp. 83–96). San Francisco, CA: Jossey-Bass.

Creswell, J. W. (2007). *Qualitative inquiry & research design: Choosing among five approaches* (2nd ed.). Thousand Oaks, CA: Sage.

Eddy, P. L., Barber, J. P., Holly, N., Brush, K., & Bohan, L. (2013). Internationalizing a campus: Bridging colonial roots to modern times. *Change Magazine, 45*(6), 43–50.

Finkelstein, M. J., Walker, E., & Chen, R. (2013). The American faculty in an age of globalization: Predictors of internationalization of research content and professional networks. *Higher Education, 66*, 325–340. doi:10.1007/s10734-012-9607-3

Fulbright. (2013). *Fulbright program in Ireland*. Retrieved from http://www.fulbright.ie/fulbright-program-in-ireland

Ganga, D., & Scott, S. (2006). Cultural "insiders" and the issue of positionality in qualitative migration research: Moving "across" and moving "along" researcher-participant divides. *Forum Qualitative Sozialforschung/Forum: Qualitative Social Research, 7*(3). Retrieved from http://www.qualitative-research.net/index.php/fqs/article/view/134

Gappa, J. M., Austin, A. E., & Trice, A. G. (2007). *Rethinking faculty work: Higher education's strategic imperative*. San Francisco, CA: Jossey-Bass.

Geertz, C. (1993). *The interpretation of cultures*. London, England: Fontana Press.

Hazelkorn, E. (2011). *Rankings and the reshaping of higher education: The battle for world-class excellence*. Hampshire, England: Palgrave Macmillan.

Higher Education Authority. (2013). *Annual Report: 2011*. Dublin, Ireland: Author. Retrieved from http://www.hea.ie/sites/default/files/hea_annual_reports_and_accounts_2011.pdf

Hurtado, S. (2007). Linking diversity with the educational and civic missions of higher education. *Review of Higher Education, 30*(2), 185–196.

Kegan, R., & Lahey, L. L. (2009). *Immunity to change: How to overcome it and unlock the potential in yourself and your organization*. Boston, MA: Harvard Business Press.

Knight, J. (2009). New developments and unintended consequences: Whither thou goest, internationalization? In R. Bhandari & S. Laughlin (Eds.), *Higher education on the move: New developments in global mobility* (pp. 113–124). New York, NY: The Institute of International Education.

Knowles, M. S. (1970). *The modern practice of adult education. Andragogy versus pedagogy.* Englewood Cliffs, NJ: Prentice-Hall.

Knowles, M. S. (1980). *The modern practice of adult education: From pedagogy to andragogy (Revised and Updated).* Englewood Cliffs, NJ: Prentice-Hall.

Merriam, S. B., & Brockett, R. G. (2007). *The profession and practice of adult education: An introduction.* San Francisco, CA: Jossey-Bass.

Organisation for Economic Co-operation and Development (OECD). (2006). *Reviews of national policies for education: Higher education in Ireland.* Paris, France: Author.

Peterson, P. M., & Helms, R. M. (2013). Internationalization revisited. *Change Magazine,* 45(2), 28–34.

Polkinghorne, D. E. (1989). Phenomenological research methods. In R. S. Valle & S. Halling (Eds.), *Existential-phenomenological perspectives in psychology: Exploring the breadth of human experience* (pp. 41–60). New York, NY: Plenum Press.

Romano, R. M. (2002). *Internationalizing the community college.* Washington, DC: Community College Press.

Van Manen, M. (1990). *Researching lived experience: Human science for an action sensitive pedagogy.* New York: State University of New York Press.

PAMELA L. EDDY is a professor of higher education at the College of William and Mary.

3

Students succeed in college by engaging with faculty, peers, and the community. Institutional leaders can utilize organizational learning strategies to learn what works to support civic learning outcomes and student success.

Civic Engagement and Organizational Learning Strategies for Student Success

Tami L. Moore, Jesse P. Mendez

Student success continues to be a pressing issue that perplexes higher education. The lack of a college degree in the global knowledge economy holds devastating effects, particularly for those at the low-socioeconomic bracket. The consequences of low numbers of degree holders are equally dire for the civic life of communities and the vitality of local and regional economies depending upon active citizens, profitable businesses, and taxpayers contributing amply to the municipal tax base. Particular impediments to access and degree completion have been identified, including lack of persistence among low-income students (Pascarella & Terenzini, 2005); academic, social, and cultural capital deficits disrupting navigation through the college experience (St. John, Hu, & Fisher, 2011; Strayhorn, 2010); and managing competing personal, professional, and academic responsibilities (Perna, 2010).

The economic potency of a college degree is substantial. The median income of individuals with a bachelor's degree is $21,700 higher than those who possess a high school diploma (College Board, 2010). In addition, college graduates have been found to have higher rates of voting (Wellman, 1999) and community volunteerism (Institute for Higher Education Policy, 2005). A college degree provides not only economic benefits but civic ones as well. Given what is at stake for individuals and communities, and the variety of barriers students face, student success remains a multifaceted, complex issue not easily addressed by one approach.

In this chapter, we argue that institutional leaders can utilize organizational learning strategies to support civic learning outcomes and student success. Civic engagement activities enhance student engagement, or "the time and effort students devote to activities that are empirically linked to desired outcomes of college *and* what institutions do to induce students

NEW DIRECTIONS FOR HIGHER EDUCATION, no. 165, Spring 2014 © 2014 Wiley Periodicals, Inc.
Published online in Wiley Online Library (wileyonlinelibrary.com) • DOI: 10.1002/he.20081

to participate in these activities" (Kuh, 2009, p. 683, italics in original; Kuh, Kinzie, Buckley, Bridges, & Hayek, 2007). Using a student engagement framework, we first explore specific questions about the impact of civic engagement on students' persistence and success, and then about changes in institutional structure and behavior necessary to advance desired student learning outcomes. Because institution type matters in the discussion of student learning outcomes, this chapter focuses specifically on student success at four-year institutions.

Student Success

Beyond the importance of degree attainment for individual students and their communities, helping students earn degrees is increasingly important for institutions of higher education in this era of performance-based funding (Dougherty, Natow, Bork, Jones, & Vega, 2013; Hearn & Holdsworth, 2002; McLendon, Hearn, & Deaton, 2006). Recently, many state legislatures have implemented systems tying state allocations to public colleges and universities to student performance (Dougherty & Reddy, 2011). For example, funding policies in Oklahoma render student success synonymous with graduation, or degree attainment (Allen, 2012), and fund institutions based on graduation rates. In actuality, student success may be most usefully defined through a wide variety of indicators.

The most common measures of success for students at four-year institutions are quantifiable: earned grade point averages, persistence to second-year enrollment, time to degree, and degree attainment. Scholar practitioners have also considered qualitative measures, including goal attainment (identified by the student and may or may not include graduation), success in subsequent coursework, academic value added through skills and knowledge acquired in coursework, appreciation for diversity and other psychosocial development indicators, citizenship skills, and self-reported student satisfaction (Crisp & Nora, 2010; Palmer, Davis, & Maramba, 2011; Perrakis & Hagedorn, 2010).

The literature on student success focuses primarily on student participants who have already enrolled in college while precluding students who never gained entry because of socioeconomic or/and family educational status. Accordingly, the current research in this area does not tell us enough about the impact on student success of the characteristics that keep many students out of college altogether. Paying attention to student background, precollege experiences, and enrollment patterns is appropriate given that these characteristics "influence to a nontrivial extent" (Kuh et al., 2007, p. 43) student enrollment decisions and their subsequent performance in college.

Student success has also been measured in terms of civic or job preparation outcomes. Previous scholars have framed these goals as somewhat mutually exclusive, from a public or a private good perspective

(McMahon, 2009). From a public good perspective, an educated society would have fewer in jail, a higher rate of literacy, lower health care costs, and better employment opportunities generating higher tax revenues for public services. The private good frame emphasizes direct benefits to individual graduates who now qualify for professional positions and will enjoy a better standard of living (Bowen, 1977; Institute for Higher Education Policy, 2005).

The context of the traditional discourse of public/private good provides a foundation for our argument at first glance. However, these frames may be "unhelpful and often confusing" (Marginson, 2007, p. 309) in the discussion of student learning outcomes given that the public/private debate is not, as Marginson argues, a zero-sum game: "the production of one kind of good provides conditions necessary to the other" (p. 310). Instead, a more useful approach would be to consider the long-term social, socioeconomic, and cultural impact of student learning, and successful achievement of the desired outcomes of a college education (Marginson, 2007). Fostering an educated citizenry fuels both the economic well-being of the United States and the civic well-being of individual communities.

Through civic engagement activities, students connect ideas from the classroom into the community and integrate their learning through cocurricular service (Smith, Nowacek, & Bernstein, 2010; see also Barber's and Wawrzynski and Baldwin's chapters in this volume for more on these ideas of integration and connectivity of learning). Civic engagement activities of all sorts are frequently referenced as powerful tools for simultaneously engaging students in the learning process, and in their communities, thereby promoting the various goals/outcomes of student engagement (Engberg & Fox, 2011; Rochford & Hock, 2010).

Civic Engagement.   *Engagement* is an oft-used term in the scholarship related to students and higher education institutions in general. Community engagement specifically involves university actors working with the communities they serve. For example, administrators engage with community leaders to advance economic development initiatives. Faculty members pursue community-engaged research agendas addressing community-identified issues. Students engage with community through service learning and other cocurricular activities referred to collectively as civic engagement (Saltmarsh & Zlotkowski, 2011; Smith et al., 2010).

Student civic engagement is both a manifestation of an institution's commitment to community engagement and an "educationally purposeful activit[y]" (Kuh et al., 2007, p. 44) through which students deepen their engagement (Kuh, 2009), and thereby enhance their chances of achieving desired learning outcomes in college, or, in other words, succeeding. Civic-minded graduates (Steinberg, Hatcher, & Bringle, 2011) will make important contributions to their communities through their capacity to generate citizen-driven solutions and through their economic activity (College Board, 2010).

Student (Academic and Social) Engagement.   The student engagement construct emphasizes the relationship between how students act and how universities support students (Kuh et al., 2007). Kuh and associates (2007) reviewed literature related to student success in college. The empirical evidence overwhelmingly confirms that student characteristics, precollege experiences, and institutional factors such as mission, size, selectivity, availability of financial aid, and structural and organizational characteristics influence student success. The bottom line: "High levels of purposeful student-faculty contact and active and collaborative learning supported by institutional environments perceived by students as inclusive and affirming are related to student satisfaction, persistence, educational attainment, and [student] learning and development across a variety of dimensions" (Kuh et al., 2007, pp. 11–12). Going forward, we use *engagement* to refer to the variety of educationally purposeful learning activities occurring in and out of the classroom, on campus, and in the community that support student psychosocial development and advance the academic and the civic missions of colleges and universities.

Engagement Supports Student Success.   Chickering and Gamson's (1987) principles of good practice in undergraduate education emphasize student–faculty contact, cooperation among students, active learning, prompt feedback, time on task for both faculty members and students, communication of high expectations, and respect for diverse talents and ways of learning. Twenty years of empirical research and longitudinal data collected through the National Survey of Student Engagement (NSSE) affirm the positive impact of these practices on student success indicators (Kuh et al., 2007). In other words, student engagement supports student learning, and this learning equates to student success (Carini, Kuh, & Klein, 2006).

Particular activities promote student learning more effectively than others. Students' interactions with their peers make the most difference in a wide range of developmental outcomes; this effect holds in both social and academic environments (Pascarella & Terenzini, 2005). The same is true for the impact of diversity experiences. Opportunities for intergroup dialogue in diverse groups are particularly valuable to promote student learning (Diaz & Perrault, 2010). Student contact with faculty also advances student participation in educationally purposeful activities in an academic environment. Both the nature and the frequency of the contact between students and their instructors and other faculty mentors matter. Students also develop interpersonal skills, self-confidence, and other attributes supporting student success by participating in cocurricular activities (Kuh et al., 2007).

To date, the discussion of student success has explored several indicators related to student retention and/or graduation, but scholars have been less vocal with regard to strategies/practices to support engagement. On the whole, institutions are lagging in their efforts to achieve student

NEW DIRECTIONS FOR HIGHER EDUCATION • DOI: 10.1002/he

success, particularly among students from traditionally underrepresented groups who are not most effectively engaged through strategies designed for a homogeneous student population (Harper & Quaye, 2009). Operationalizing the focus on student learning outcomes will require transformative changes in the way university institutional actors understand and enact the institution's responsibility for creating conditions to foster success for all students.

This chapter is grounded in three interdependent assumptions, nested in organizational learning principles. First, following engagement theory, student learning/success is the shared responsibility of individual students who must engage and institutional leaders who must establish and maintain structures and programming to support engagement by an increasingly diverse student body (Harper & Quaye, 2009; Kuh et al., 2007). Second, students deepen their engagement with faculty, their peers, and the community through civic engagement activities, and in doing so they develop as citizens (Engberg & Fox, 2011; Warren, 2012). Third, institutional leaders can utilize organizational learning strategies to learn what works to institutionalize civic engagement and therein support student success.

Colleges and universities can have a tremendous impact on student success, but this path poses logistical challenges. Institutional leaders should reflect on their own approaches to teaching and student success, and commit to supporting endeavors that promote student learning. This requires, first and foremost, expanding definitions of student success to intentionally focus on the intended outcomes of a college education before operationalizing these definitions in campus-wide programming and services. For institutions considering navigating these waters, civic engagement provides multifaceted benefits, not just limited to community well-being, but also student engagement, student success, and state support through performance-based-funding initiatives. Institutions that choose this path must demonstrate a willingness to engage in robust organizational learning challenges.

Organizational Learning

Organizational learning provides higher education administrators tools to strengthen their institution's efforts to support student engagement and, thereby, student learning and success. Organizational learning is a neutral, reflective process through which an organization, and/or its actors, process(es) information and exhibit(s) changes in thinking or behavior (Kezar, 2005a, 2005b). Anderson (2005) supports the adoption of an organizational learning approach to foster community–university partnerships. We build on her ideas to argue for organizational learning to support student success, particularly as it is improved through civic engagement activities. Although there is broad agreement among scholars about the positive impacts of civic engagement on academic, personal, social, and citizenship outcomes for students (Engberg & Fox, 2011), institutions on the whole remain slow to institutionalize community–university engagement. Organizational learning could foster the institutionalization of civic engagement in support of student learning.

Defining Organizational Learning.   Scholars disagree about what constitutes learning for organizations or their individual actors, and whether the organization, unique from individual institutional actors, can be said to learn (Kezar, 2005b). The outcome of that debate does not limit the "processes for acquiring information, interpreting data, developing knowledge, and sustaining learning" (Kezar, 2005a, p. 13) offered in an organizational context. An institutional environment ripe for employing organizational learning strategies "promotes a culture of learning, [conceptualizes employees as] a community of learners, and . . . ensures that individual learning enriches and enhances the organization as a whole" (Kezar, 2005a, p. 10). Universities provide such an environment.

Key organizational learning practices include adopting a system's perspective, presenting mental models reflecting a new understanding of the institution; supporting individuals within the institution to develop personal mastery of relevant knowledge; and expanding their capacity for personal growth. By modeling reflexive practice, institutional leaders encourage individual faculty and administrators to reflect not only on what they are learning about how students at their institution engage and the outcomes of this engagement, but also on how this information can be utilized to refine or improve those interactions.

Adopting an organizational learning framework offers promise for expanding reflexive practice informed by constituent feedback, and improving civic engagement experiences, and student success outcomes for students. Extant feedback loops need more attention for fostering reflexive practice and gathering constituent input. At present, administrators assume that students and faculty can provide feedback about current civic/engagement initiatives. Students communicate directly through course evaluations and indirectly through their success statistics. Mechanisms for faculty input exist in their performance evaluations, and the shared governance process, allowing opportunities to shape university structure and influence the design of support structures as needed. But the structures for community feedback are severely underdeveloped (Anderson, 2005), largely because knowledge emerging from the community is undervalued in higher education. The persistence of this culture denigrates student success, or at the least does not value learning that occurs outside the classroom, despite the demonstrated links between civic engagement, student engagement, and student success indicators (Carini et al., 2006; Engberg & Fox, 2011).

Institutional leaders can construct mental models to support a new institutional culture and practice that intentionally supports civic engagement and student success as a whole. Existing mental models, the internal frameworks guiding action by the institution and individuals within it, "must be identified, scrutinized, and when necessary, reconceptualized" (Anderson, 2005, p. 43). Single-loop learning processes can be used for the work of identifying and scrutinizing the internal framework. Double-loop learning allows the institution to draw on what it learns to inform the reconceptualization of the mental model guiding student success initiatives.

Several examples of organizational learning supporting student success exist in the community–university engagement literature. Lounsbury and Pollack (2001) discuss "shifting logics and . . . [a] cultural repackaging of service-learning" (p. 319) as part of the move at many colleges and universities to institutionalize civic engagement. Reviewing several decades of the magazine *Change in Higher Education,* the authors identified "logics" (Lounsbury & Pollack, 2001, p. 323) explaining the shift from closed to open-system thinking in higher education that began in the early 1980s. Talk of shifting logics is another way of discussing the reconceptualization of the system, an example of an organizational learning exercise. Organizations learned to incorporate aspects of service learning and civic engagement and changed their practices; the shift in focus from solving social problems to serving discipline-specific learning goals became evident around 1982 and continues today (Saltmarsh & Zlotkowski, 2011).

Promoting a Culture of Organizational Learning. Elements of institutional culture and organizational structure can either promote or inhibit organizational learning (Kezar, 2005a). Characteristics such as decentralized governance, trust among institutional actors at different levels of the institutional hierarchy, and rewards, associated with higher education institutions, promote organizational learning. One approach to realizing the potential of organizational learning is, then, to foster a culture of learning within the organization (Anderson, 2005). Ramaley (2000) has written about her experiences as president of the University of Vermont and of Portland State University (Ramaley & Holland, 2005), leading transformational change aimed at opening each of these institutions more fully to interaction with the communities they serve. At both institutions, senior campus leaders framed transformative change as a scholarly act. Many who would be involved in designing and implementing the change were trained as scholars; Ramaley and Holland describe the scholars as more likely to support what they considered warranted changes, identified through a rigorous process including as much empirical evidence as available, and the impact evaluated through a scholarly process. Framing change as a scholarly act, while not explicit to organizational learning, represents a way to engage faculty more willingly in the process of institutional change.

Implications for Practice

We have argued in the previous sections that first, civic engagement supports student engagement and student success, and second, the promotion of a culture of learning can institutionalize the organizational learning process. Holistically, the university must attend to creating a supportive learning environment for all students despite their background, with appropriate opportunities for students to engage inside and outside the classroom. The university's responsibility in this equation becomes more complex as the student body becomes more diverse, thereby rendering previously appropriate assumptions of student homogeneity now inappropriate (Harper & Quaye, 2009). Universities cannot simply maintain the status quo; rather, they must give attention to the experiences and developmental needs of a diverse student body when designing programs and services. To do so will require the organization, or its institutional actors, to learn new ways of understanding students, and more current "educationally effective practices" (Kuh et al., 2007, p. 43). In order for the institutional culture to embrace and facilitate organizational learning, institutional leaders can frame cultural change as a scholarly act to appeal to the faculty and to induce their buy-in. Some institutions may consider conducting a cultural audit of current practices and attitudes not only of faculty and administrators but also of undergraduate students toward student success and civic engagement, providing a baseline for these dialogues. In addition, state policymakers and community leaders, another lot of stakeholders, should be not only informed but also involved and invested in this cultural adjustment. Although there is no clear path for institutions to adopt organizational learning to induce civic engagement, the one prerequisite to this process is broadening our understanding of student success.

References

Allen, S. (2012, April 19). Oklahoma System of Higher Education looks to move to performance-based funding. *The Oklahoman*. Retrieved from http://newsok.com/oklahoma-system-of-higher-education-looks-to-move-to-performance-based-funding/article/3667579

Anderson, J. L. (2005). Community service as learning. In A. Kezar (Ed.), *New Directions for Higher Education: No. 131. Organizational learning in higher education* (pp. 37–48). San Francisco, CA: Jossey-Bass.

Bowen, H. (1977). *Investment in learning: The individual and social value of American higher education*. San Francisco, CA: Jossey-Bass.

Carini, R. M., Kuh, G. D., & Klein, S. P. (2006). Student engagement and student learning: Testing the linkages. *Research in Higher Education, 47*(1), 1–32. doi:10.1007/s11162–005–8150–9

Chickering, A. W., & Gamson, Z. F. (1987). Seven principles for good practice in undergraduate education. *AAHE Bulletin, 39*(7), 3–7.

College Board. (2010). *Education pays: The benefits of higher education for individuals and society*. Washington, DC: Author. Retrieved from http://trends.collegeboard.org/education-pays

Crisp, G., & Nora, A. (2010). Hispanic student success: Factors influencing the persistence and transfer decisions of Latino community college students enrolled in developmental education. *Research in Higher Education, 51*(2), 175–194.

Diaz, A., & Perrault, R. (2010). Sustained dialogue and civic life: Post-college impacts. *Michigan Journal of Community Service Learning, 17*(1), 32–43.

Dougherty, K., Natow, R., Bork, R., Jones, S., & Vega, B. (2013). Accounting for higher education accountability: Political origins of state performance funding for higher education. *Teachers College Record, 115*(1). Retrieved from http://www.tcrecord.org/content.asp?contentid=16741

Dougherty, K. J., & Reddy, V. (2011). *The impacts of state performance funding systems on higher education institutions: Research literature review and policy recommendations.* New York, NY: Community College Research Center, Teachers College, Columbia University. Retrieved from http://ccrc.tc.columbia.edu/Publication.asp?UID=1004

Engberg, M., & Fox, K. (2011). Exploring the relationship between undergraduate service-learning experiences and global perspective-taking. *Journal of Student Affairs Research and Practice, 48*(1), 85–105.

Harper, S. R., & Quaye, S. J. (2009). *Student engagement in higher education: Theoretical perspectives and practical approaches for diverse populations.* New York, NY: Routledge.

Hearn, J. C., & Holdsworth, J. M. (2002). Influences of state-level policies and practices on college students' learning. *Peabody Journal of Education, 77*(3), 6–39.

Institute for Higher Education Policy. (2005). *The investment payoff: A 50-state analysis of the public and private benefits of higher education.* Washington, DC: Author.

Kezar, A. (2005a). What campuses need to know about organizational learning and the learning organization. In A. Kezar (Ed.), *New Directions for Higher Education: No. 131. Organizational learning in higher education* (pp. 7–22). San Francisco, CA: Jossey-Bass.

Kezar, A. (2005b). What do we mean by "learning" in the context of higher education? In A. Kezar (Ed.), *New Directions for Higher Education: No. 131. Organizational learning in higher education* (pp. 49–59). San Francisco, CA: Jossey-Bass.

Kuh, G. D. (2009). What student affairs professionals need to know about student engagement. *Journal of College Student Development, 50*(6), 683–706.

Kuh, G. D., Kinzie, J., Buckley, J. A., Bridges, B. K., & Hayek, J. C. (2007). Piecing together the student success puzzle. *ASHE/Higher Education Report, 32*(5), 1–182.

Lounsbury, M., & Pollack, S. (2001). Institutionalizing civic engagement: Shifting logics and the cultural repackaging of service-learning in US higher education. *Organization, 8*(2), 319–339.

Marginson, S. (2007). The public/private divide in higher education: A global revision. *Higher Education, 53*, 307–333. doi:10.1007/s10734–005–8230-y

McLendon, M. K., Hearn, J. C., & Deaton, R. (2006). Called to account: Analyzing the origins and spread of state performance-accountability policies for higher education. *Educational Evaluation and Policy Analysis, 28*(1), 1–24.

McMahon, W. W. (2009). *Higher learning, greater good: The private and social benefits of higher education.* Baltimore, MD: John Hopkins University Press.

Palmer, R. T., Davis, R. J., & Maramba, D. C. (2011). The impact of family support on the success of black men at an historically black university: Affirming the revision of Tinto's theory. *Journal of College Student Development, 52*(5), 577–597.

Pascarella, E. T., & Terenzini, P. T. (2005). *How college affects students: Vol. 2. A 3rd decade of research.* San Francisco, CA: Jossey-Bass.

Perna, L. W. (2010). *Understanding the working college student: New research and its implications for policy and practice.* Sterling, VA: Stylus.

Perrakis, A., & Hagedorn, L. S. (2010). Latino/a student success in community colleges and Hispanic-serving institution status. *Community College Journal of Research and Practice, 34*(10), 797–813.

Ramaley, J. A. (2000). Change as a scholarly act: Higher education research transfer to practice. In A. Kezar & P. Eckel (Eds.), *New Directions for Higher Education: No. 110. Moving beyond the gap between research and practice in higher education* (pp. 75–88). San Francisco, CA: Jossey-Bass.

Ramaley, J. A., & Holland, B. H. (2005). Modeling learning: The role of leaders. In A. Kezar (Ed.), *New Directions for Higher Education: No. 131. Organizational learning in higher education* (pp. 75–86). San Francisco, CA: Jossey-Bass.

Rochford, R. A., & Hock, S. (2010). A letter-writing campaign: Linking academic success and civic engagement. *Journal of Community Engagement and Scholarship, 3*(2), 76–83.

Saltmarsh, J., & Zlotkowski, E. (2011). *Higher education and democracy: Essays on service-learning and civic engagement.* Philadelphia, PA: Temple University Press.

Smith, M. B., Nowacek, R. S., & Bernstein, J. L. (2010). *Citizenship across the curriculum.* Bloomington: Indiana University Press.

Steinberg, K., Hatcher, J. A., & Bringle, R. G. (2011). Civic minded graduate: A north star. *Michigan Journal of Community Service Learning, 18*(1), 19–33.

St. John, E. P., Hu, S., & Fisher, A. S. (2011). *Breaking through the access barrier: How academic capital formation can improve policy in higher education.* New York, NY: Routledge.

Strayhorn, T. L. (2010). When race and gender collide: Social and cultural capital's influence on the academic achievement of African American and Latino males. *The Review of Higher Education, 33*(3), 307–332.

Warren, J. L. (2012). Does service-learning increase student learning?: A meta-analysis. *Michigan Journal of Community Service Learning, 18*(2), 56–61.

Wellman, J. V. (1999). *Contributing to the civic good: Assessing and accounting for the civic contributions of higher education (Report).* Washington, DC: The Institute for Higher Education Policy.

TAMI L. MOORE is an assistant professor of higher education and student affairs and program coordinator of higher education and college student development at Oklahoma State University.

JESSE P. MENDEZ is an associate professor of higher education and student affairs and school head of School of Educational Studies at Oklahoma State University.

4

This chapter proposes a simple framework, "orthogonality," to help clarify what stakeholders think about learning in college, how we assess outcomes, and how clear assessment methods might help increase confidence in returns on investment.

"Orthogonality" in Learning and Assessment

David Leslie

Recent articles (Arum & Roksa, 2011) and press coverage (Carey, 2012) focus popular opinion—and therefore that of policy makers—on the impression that colleges and universities rip off the public due to low expectations and standards for learning, high tuition, and plenty of diversion for undergraduates beyond the classroom. The disconnect between contemporary accreditation standards requiring assessment of outcomes and what the public thinks about learning in college belies over 70 years of conceptual progress (Penn, 2011) in measuring both the array of collegiate outcomes and the design of value-added studies. See also, for example, work of Astin and Antonio (2012), Dressel (1976), and Pace (1979).

Popular concern with the cost of college, default rates on student loans, campus safety, lengthening time-to-degree trends, and lower graduation rates may divert attention from the subtler issues regarding quality of education. In fact, the U.S. Department of Education's College Affordability and Transparency Center's new "College Scorecard" offers comparative data on many of these dimensions, but none at all on "quality" (U.S. Department of Education, 2013). In the end, colleges and universities struggle to sustain their focus on quality and how to assess what students learn (and take from their college experiences).

Many initiatives at institutions (e.g., Alverno College, 2013), associations (e.g., Association of American Colleges and Universities, 2013), foundations (e.g., The Teagle Foundation, 2013), institutes (e.g., National Institute for Learning Outcomes Assessment, 2013), and national organizations (e.g., Council for Higher Education Accreditation, 2013) promote the assessment of higher education quality. Supporting this focus on quality, accrediting organizations now require that institutions assess student outcomes. But few would argue that conceptual or practical consensus has

NEW DIRECTIONS FOR HIGHER EDUCATION, no. 165, Spring 2014 © 2014 Wiley Periodicals, Inc.
Published online in Wiley Online Library (wileyonlinelibrary.com) • DOI: 10.1002/he.20082

been achieved on either the intended outcomes of "college," or on how to represent quality (comparative or absolute) to those who pay or to those intending to hire graduates.

Thomas Friedman (2013), in a widely quoted column, recently pointed out that the electronic revolution (e.g., MOOCs, Google) has rendered commonly taught content as less relevant. Instead, the focus is now on how learning itself occurs and the application of transferable skills. Friedman predicts that the old model of accumulating credit hours in conventional classes may quickly shift to a more fluid set of learning experiences in which outcomes—rather than credits—are the most important criterion.

Leaders of institutions may need a more compelling framework to support articulation of what outcomes to expect, how to assess those outcomes, and—as importantly—how to communicate with the policy community and public about what they get in return for investing in higher education. This chapter proposes to lay out a simple framework, "orthogonality," to help clarify what stakeholders think about learning in college, how we assess outcomes, and how clear assessment methods might help increase confidence in returns on investment in higher education.

Orthogonal outcomes are those—such as use of inductive logic—that can (and should) be taught and experienced across all (or most) of the curriculum (and reinforced via the extracurriculum as well). The challenge for leaders (and the goal of this chapter) is to bring convergence and consensus about orthogonal outcomes and to develop ways these outcomes can best be learned and assessed.

Stakeholder Demands for Learning

Historically, the goals of higher education have transmogrified from producing religious leaders to a broad array of intellectual, professional, occupational, and personal outcomes. There is no obviously "universal" set of learning goals. General education, liberal education, higher order skills, literacy, STEM skills, leadership, values, and an ever-expanding inventory of overarching, cross-cutting rubrics have both helped to clarify and to muddle just what students should know and be able to do when they achieve a baccalaureate degree.

As representative as any set, the Association of American Colleges and Universities proposes that all students progressively learn:

Knowledge of Human Cultures and the Physical and Natural World

- Through study in the sciences and mathematics, social sciences, humanities, histories, languages, and the arts

Focused by engagement with big questions, both contemporary and enduring

NEW DIRECTIONS FOR HIGHER EDUCATION • DOI: 10.1002/he

Intellectual and Practical Skills, Including

- Inquiry and analysis
- Critical and creative thinking
- Written and oral communication
- Quantitative literacy
- Information literacy
- Teamwork and problem solving

Practiced extensively, across the curriculum, in the context of progressively more challenging problems, projects, and standards for performance

Personal and Social Responsibility, Including

- Civic knowledge and engagement—local and global
- Intercultural knowledge and competence
- Ethical reasoning and action
- Foundations and skills for lifelong learning

Anchored through active involvement with diverse communities and real-world challenges

Integrative and Applied Learning, Including

- Synthesis and advanced accomplishment across general and specialized studies

Demonstrated through the application of knowledge, skills, and responsibilities to new settings and complex problems

(Association of American Colleges and Universities, 2013, http://www .aacu.org/leap/vision.cfm)

See also http://www.p21.org/storage/documents/P21_Framework_Defini tions.pdf for the 21st Century Skills recommended for all students.

Where and how these important things can be learned and how students' progress, individually and collectively, can be monitored are topics that AAC&U continues to address. As enduring as these outcomes may seem, higher education has always adapted and changed to an increasingly complex social, cultural, and economic context. So what may be a goal in one era—religious leadership in colonial times, for example—can readily be superseded by others—mathematical and scientific leadership during the Cold War era. And curricular design—arranging experiences to cause intended learning—has morphed over time from rote exercises (Yale Report) to electives (Charles W. Eliot) to MOOCs. Institutions also change their roles—Florida's community colleges now offer four-year degrees as "state colleges." Formerly religious institutions now offer secular studies and vocational training (e.g., William Penn University in Iowa, founded by Quakers, now offers a "college for working adults" on a separate campus). And most institutions now try to expose their students to international experiences. The Institute of International Education (2012) reports that nearly 274,000 students at U.S. colleges received credit for study abroad in 2011.

Students and faculty also change from generation to generation. What students know; how they learn; and where, when, and how their development proceeds have all changed dramatically in a few short decades. (I never saw television until I was in third grade; I never used a computer until I learned FORTRAN and how to punch cards in graduate school; I had to retrieve books and articles physically in library stacks even after I had tenure.)

In other words, all the elements in teaching, learning, and assessment are moving in a constant, kaleidoscopic whirl. The challenge is to bring some kind of coherence to what happens during students' undergraduate experience, and to show the public that returns on its investment have borne intended fruits.

Assessment of Learning—Orthogonality Defined

What should all college graduates know and be able to do—independently of majors or concentrations? Are there sets of knowledge and skills that cross disciplines and professions? What do educated citizens share in terms of values and understandings? Questions like these suggest that the college experience should result in outcomes that are common to all, that physics majors, art majors, and nursing majors should be equally competent in ways of analyzing, thinking, creating, and contributing to their families, communities, cultures, societies, professions, and humanity.

Common outcomes, if all students should achieve them, are "orthogonal" to outcomes that are specific to majors or concentrations. Table 4.1 shows a rudimentary way of thinking orthogonally about outcomes.

Tabulating outcomes both vertically and horizontally emphasizes a way to connect both generic and specific outcomes through experiences. Obviously, the individual cells in Table 4.1 would be filled as faculty and students work out what each classroom experience, like "disconfirming immersion," might mean in each discipline. In physics, for example, one might consider how important figures were influenced by culture as they grappled with fundamental problems. Why might Archimedes have been the one to understand displacement? Because Greeks had baths? Or in biology, why was Darwin's perspective on the origin of species more readily accepted in some communities than in others? Because biblical faith was at the core of some cultures' values, but less so in others?

NEW DIRECTIONS FOR HIGHER EDUCATION • DOI: 10.1002/he

Table 4.1. Orthogonal and Generic Outcomes of "College"

	Physics	Literature	Nursing	Sociology	Orthogonal Outcomes, General to All Students
Puzzle Solving					Inductive reasoning
Case Studies					Ethical reasoning
Disconfirming Immersion					Cross-cultural competence
Data Generation and Analysis					Quantitative skill
Outcomes Specific to Majors	Understanding "force"	Writing criticism	Recognizing symptoms	Comparing social roles	

Without trying to fill in all the blanks, because Table 4.1 is only illustrative, not exhaustive, nor drawn from any institution's existing array of outcomes, the matrix sets up a challenge. If an institution claims to be producing "orthogonal" outcomes (right-hand column), has it designed ways (left-hand column) in which all students can achieve them across their fields of concentration? More to the point, can the institution show evidence that these outcomes are being attained?

Design.   Alexander Astin's (Astin & Antonio, 2012) work on value-added design of college education is helpful in both its simplicity and its power. Over many years and publications, Astin constructed a theoretical linkage among student "Input" characteristics, the "Environmental" and "Experiential" qualities of a particular campus and its curricula, and the change that might be measured between students' states at admission and their states at graduation ("Outcomes"). This I-E-O model can be used in an imaginative way to fill the cells in Table 4.1.

I think an institution grappling with orthogonality might approach the assessment design problem in two phases: the self-reflection phase and the distillation phase. Once an assessment plan is created, it would be followed by an experimentation phase.

Self-Reflection.   Institutions cannot be all things to all people (Leslie & Fretwell, 1996). With limited resources, pressures from the marketplace, and context with a given faculty, student body, alumni support, and public image, an institution simply must make strategic accommodation in a "satisficing" (Simon, 1997, p. 118) way. To build consensus, it is probably best to begin with a challenge to the entire community in thinking (debating, contesting) about core values, goals, and outcomes *within the real constraints of time, place, and resources.* But this level of self-assessment gives all stakeholders opportunities to put ideas on the table about (a) what outcomes an institution should want its students to demonstrate and (b) what "E's"—experiences and environmental factors—should be applied toward those ends independently of demands in specific concentrations.

Deep differences about what outcomes are worth supporting may be expected. An article in the *Chronicle of Higher Education* (Schmidt, 2013) outlines a substantial difference of opinion between the National Association of Scholars and Bowdoin College. The Association alleges that Bowdoin's curriculum overemphasizes matters of gender, ethnicity, and social justice while "neglecting instruction about Western civilization" (Schmidt, 2013, "A Vibrant Organization," para. 2). In the polarized political atmosphere of the times, particular attention to the legitimacy—public and private acceptability—of whatever outcomes an institution proposes to pursue may make or break the effort. How constituencies and markets see these outcomes can generate greater support or set a backlash in motion. So both the substance and the communication of the desired outcome efforts demand close attention.

NEW DIRECTIONS FOR HIGHER EDUCATION • DOI: 10.1002/he

Distillation.   At each institution, the likely array of "E's" and "O's" will be broad, conflicting, overlapping, and perhaps even inconsistent with each other. So distilling this array into something consistent, workable, and acceptable to core stakeholders will require an intense second phase of planning. This phase has to achieve buy-in, so it has to be collaborative; no dean or provost or president can expect the community to accept *ex cathedra* dictation, but leaders must also be prepared to accelerate closure in what will inevitably be a contentious process (Kotter & Cohen, 2002).

Most institutions already implicitly or explicitly support orthogonal educational and developmental goals for their students, but they may not be equally successful at assessing outcomes or in using assessment as feedback in efforts at continuous improvement. Yet, experience is critical in a collective effort to converge on what is worthwhile and on what is workable. In this regard, "distillation" should be a continuous process, monitoring the values of those the institution wishes to engage; understanding the successes and failures of courses, programs, and experiences in supporting common goals; and engaging in continuous (open) dialogue about what is important and what has—or has not—worked.

Parsimony is a virtue. In a community of active, vigorous minds, competition for preferred values can lead to indiscriminate acceptance of too many goals. An ethic of cooperation and consensus—certainly an important desideratum in an academic community—can override the process of distillation. It is probably better to start simply, experimentally, tentatively and to focus on fewer rather than more prospective goals and outcomes. Perhaps the process can be forced into a relatively simple framework, as outlined in Table 4.1, that can serve as a way of setting boundaries.

Disciplined (not "disciplinary!") orthogonality requires practice and experience. The most difficult issue may be asking faculty to "share" classroom time between orthogonal goals (such as inductive thinking) and disciplinary substance and content. The whole point of orthogonality, though, is to use learning experiences synergistically. Laws of motion in physics can be taught experientially and inductively so students are learning both skills and content knowledge simultaneously.

Connecting "E" With "O"

It is beyond the scope of a short chapter to deal in any depth with assessing orthogonal outcomes. This process is a highly technical issue, so I will only try to propose a framework for discussion. To return to *I-E-O* (Astin & Antonio, 2012), Table 4.1 sets up a cause–effect hypothesis: Experiences "E" (of a particular kind) produce outcomes "O" (of a certain kind). How strong those linkages may be lies at the heart of any legitimate design. Many institutions try venturesome new experiences for their students (e.g., study abroad, interning, and online exercises) without necessarily connecting them to outcomes. Similarly, many institutions tout powerful outcomes without designing experiences that should help students achieve them. The fact that the public and students place merit in these claims is evident in recent court cases in which students have sued universities for failing to fulfill promises (see, e.g., Hirst, 2013; Palazzolo & Smith, 2013).

While powerful experiences may be valuable in themselves, institutions should provide evidence that those experiences do produce intended outcomes. The starting point in assessing orthogonal outcomes has to be connecting what students do and what they learn. It is far easier (but not "easy") to test students for content (solving equations) than it is to test them to see if they can construct quantitatively imaginative analyses in ambiguous situations and to find evidence showing how they learned to do it.

Designing a Plan.   If cause–effect can be established as a first-order desideratum, assessing outcomes then will involve a fairly straightforward pathway through a set of common steps. A series of guiding questions can help identify the type of assessment plan to create to determine if students have acquired orthogonal skills:

1. Is the assessment to be a "test"? Or based on observation of behavior (authenticity)?
2. Is the assessment to be standardized versus specific for some population of students? Or particular to individual students (as, for example, in an oral examination for a thesis project)?
3. Will behavior be assessed against a criterion (must show explicit behaviors or knowledge) or against a norm (usually stated as exceeding a given percentile in a defined population)?
4. How will a sample of learning experiences and outcome behaviors be developed? Will all students be assessed, or will a sampling suffice?
5. How will the usual technical standards for testing (e.g., reliability, validity) be met?

Existing surveys and tests may well satisfy an institution's interest in orthogonality, but only to a point. What one institution considers "ethical reasoning" may not be relevant to another. So off-the-shelf methods will not fit all cases—and may, in fact, be misapplied unless there is a clear relationship between instrument, design of student experiences, and outcome. In fact, one of the most common instruments, the National Survey of Student Engagement, emphasizes experiences that may or may not be part of an institution's affirmative design to achieve orthogonality. (See critiques of NSSE in Campbell & Cabrera, 2011.)

Feedback.   Orthogonality goes beyond conventional outcome-oriented plans because, in purest form, it should focus attention on "how" learning is stimulated and encouraged. Instead of constructing a curriculum around content and instructional modules, an orthogonally designed curriculum *crosses* subject matter lines to concentrate on process. So, if mastering inductive reasoning is an outcome, and puzzle solving is a means to that end, the design of cumulative learning experiences should cross subject matter areas to develop increasingly sophisticated puzzle solving independently of subject matter.

Whatever feedback may be generated on learning processes and outcomes will have to cross the typical "silos" of departmental major fields. In the case of inductive reasoning (the outcome), faculty will want to understand what puzzle-solving exercises (the experience) result in what kinds of skills in inductive reasoning. So physics, literature, art, and business should share in developing progressively advanced puzzle solving, as well as in learning collaboratively about what works to advance students' inductive reasoning behaviors.

Conclusion: Building the Narrative

However assessment is done, the results of an orthogonally organized curriculum should feed back into the refinement and advancement of the connections between students' learning experiences and the intended results. If this process is open and collaborative, it should help an institution converge on a clear narrative about the value of its efforts: "This is what we do, how we do it, and the results we get affirm we are on the right track." A clear narrative of this kind is far better than the usual platitudes that are unsubstantiated by evidence. The effort itself should help credibility with both the public and with the institution's accreditors. The narrative can distinguish the institution in a broad sea of claims about higher education and its effectiveness. But more importantly, knowing what an institution is about, knowing how to get the results it expects, and working across traditional lines to get those results can enrich graduates' lives with sets of skills and understandings so important to their own lives and to their contributions to society.

References

Alverno College. (2013). *The eight core abilities*. Retrieved from http://www.alverno.edu/academics/ouruniquecurriculum/the8coreabilities/

Arum, R., & Roksa, J. (2011). *Academically adrift: Limited learning on college campuses*. Chicago, IL: University of Chicago Press.

Association of American Colleges and Universities. (2013). *Liberal Education and America's Promise (LEAP): Essential learning outcomes*. Retrieved from http://www.aacu.org/leap/vision.cfm

Astin, A. W., & Antonio, A. L. (2012). *Assessment for excellence: The philosophy and practice of assessment and evaluation in higher education*. Lanham, MD: Rowman & Littlefield.

Campbell, C. M., & Cabrera, A. F. (2011). How sound is NSSE?: Investigating the psychometric properties of NSSE at a public, research-extensive institution. *The Review of Higher Education, 35*(1), 77–103.

Carey, K. (2012, December 9). Who will hold colleges accountable? *The New York Times*. Retrieved from http://www.nytimes.com/2012/12/10/opinion/who-will-hold-colleges-accountable.html?_r=0

Council for Higher Education Accreditation. (2013). Retrieved from http://www.chea .org/

Dressel, P. L. (1976). *Handbook of academic evaluation*. San Francisco, CA: Jossey-Bass.

Friedman, T. (2013, March 5). The professors' big stage. *The New York Times*. Retrieved from http://www.nytimes.com/2013/03/06/opinion/friedman-the-professors-big-stage .html?_r=0

Hirst, E. J. (2013, March 1). Concordia students say degrees not what they paid for. *Chicago Tribune*. Retrieved from http://articles.chicagotribune.com/2013-03-01 /news/chi-students-sue-over-lesser-degrees-so-much-time-20130228_1_accreditation -concordia-students-graduate-program

Institute of International Education. (2012). *Open Doors*® *2012 "Fast Facts."* Retrieved from http://www.iie.org/en/Research-and-Publications/Open-Doors

Kotter, J., & Cohen, D. (2002). *The heart of change*. Boston, MA: Harvard Press.

Leslie, D. W., & Fretwell, E. K., Jr. (1996). *Wise moves in hard times*. San Francisco, CA: Jossey-Bass.

National Institute for Learning Outcomes Assessment. (2013). Retrieved from http://www.learningoutcomeassessment.org/

Pace, C. R. (1979). *Measuring outcomes of college: Fifty years of findings and recommendations for the future*. San Francisco, CA: Jossey-Bass.

Palazzolo, J., & Smith, J. (2013, March 10). Some grads face longer odds: Law schools lacking ABA accreditation put students under a tough job hurdle. *Wall Street Journal*. Retrieved from http://online.wsj.com/article/SB1000142412788732 4096404578352473272923326.html

Penn, J. D. (2011). The case for assessing complex general education student learning outcomes. In J. Penn (Ed.), *New Directions for Institutional Research: No. 149. Assessing complex general education student learning outcomes* (pp. 5–14). San Francisco, CA: Jossey-Bass.

Schmidt, P. (2013, March 4). National association of scholars joins investor in teeing up a critique of Bowdoin. *The Chronicle of Higher Education*. Retrieved from http://chronicle.com/article/National-Association-of/137669/

Simon, H. A. (1997). *Administrative behavior: A study of decision-making processes in administrative organizations* (4th ed.). New York, NY: Free Press.

The Teagle Foundation. (2013). Retrieved from http://www.teaglefoundation.org/

U.S. Department of Education. (2013). *College scorecard*. Retrieved from http://collegecost.ed.gov/scorecard/index.aspx

DAVID LESLIE *is Chancellor Professor of Education (Emeritus) at the College of William & Mary.*

NEW DIRECTIONS FOR HIGHER EDUCATION • DOI: 10.1002/he

5

High-impact learning practices can connect varied elements of the college environment to create a more coherent educational experience that facilitates student learning.

Promoting High-Impact Student Learning: Connecting Key Components of the Collegiate Experience

Matthew Wawrzynski, Roger Baldwin

Two landmark publications near the end of the 20th century (Barr & Tagg, 1995; Chickering & Gamson, 1991) caused many stakeholders in higher education to pause and take a closer look at undergraduate student learning. Up to this time, much professional literature focused primarily on strategies to improve teaching practices with little attention specifically on learning outcomes. These two influential documents spurred many conversations on campuses and at professional conferences, and many books and articles have been written on methods colleges and universities can employ to promote student learning more effectively. Subsequently, other authors (e.g., Keeling, 2006; Kuh, 2005, 2008) have encouraged higher education professionals to expand their focus to include the broader context where students learn by mapping their institution's entire learning environment (Borrego, 2006; Keeling, 2006). A comprehensive learning map should include internships, student organizations, living environments, work-study jobs, study abroad programs, and other places where students learn in addition to traditional learning sites such as classrooms and laboratories.

Ideally, all dimensions of the college experience contribute to student learning and development. An array of college experiences, ranging from formal classroom to cocurricular activities, have the potential to motivate, facilitate, and/or reinforce student learning during college and engage students in high-impact learning opportunities (AAC&U, 2007). However, too often key elements of the college experience are disconnected and not mutually reinforcing. Many students see college as separate systems for learning (i.e., academic classroom and cocurricular experiences). In the process, opportunities are lost to bolster, deepen, and generalize learning beyond the immediate setting where it occurs.

New Directions for Higher Education, no. 165, Spring 2014 © 2014 Wiley Periodicals, Inc.
Published online in Wiley Online Library (wileyonlinelibrary.com) • DOI: 10.1002/he.20083

51

Missing from many of the conversations around student learning is a discussion of strategies institutions and educators can use to help students connect the learning that occurs in the different facets of their college experience. This chapter examines the collegiate learning environment through the lenses of the literature on high-impact practices (AAC&U, 2007; Brownell & Swaner, 2010) and transformative learning (Cranton, 2006; Mezirow, 2000). High-impact practices (e.g., first-year seminars and experiences, common intellectual experiences, learning communities, writing-intensive courses, collaborative assignments and projects, undergraduate research, diversity/global learning, service learning, internships, and capstone courses and projects; Kuh, 2008) in particular provide a space in which authentic learning occurs and opportunities for transformative learning are possible. We consider how high-impact practices (HIPs) can be used to connect the varied elements of the college environment in pursuit of a more coherent educational experience that facilitates learning across the college years and yields maximum benefit for students. Our goal is to encourage educators throughout higher education to see the various roles they can play in building an integrated collegiate environment that promotes connected learning and takes full advantage of the wide range of learning opportunities their college or university offers to its students.

Mapping the Collegiate Learning Environment

George Kuh and his coauthors (Kuh, 2005) in their book, *Student Success in College,* report that colleges and universities known for promoting success share responsibility for student learning widely. These institutions recognize that student learning occurs in multiple collegiate venues and is not solely the domain of the formal academic program. Kuh and his colleagues concluded, "Student success must be everyone's business in order to create the conditions that encourage and support students to engage in educationally productive activities..." (p. 295), arguing that "the value of the out-of-class experience to student success cannot be overestimated" (p. 296). Like other high-performing organizations, colleges and universities must employ partnerships, cross-functional collaborations, and responsive units to achieve their objectives, including enhanced learning, the overarching goal of higher education (Kuh, 2005).

In *Learning Reconsidered 2*, Borrego (2006) asserts that the "entire campus is a learning community" (p. 11). According to Borrego's vision, all elements of an educational community, not just professors and academic resources, should be aligned to facilitate and reinforce students' learning. Full utilization of the rich learning environment most colleges and universities provide, however, requires a clear picture of the places where learning occurs on the physical campus and through other affiliated programs and educational settings both online and off-campus. Borrego

(2006) advocates mapping the learning environment by "recognizing, identifying, and documenting the sites for learning activities" (p. 11) an institution offers. Mapping can be a key step in a strategy to leverage an institution's programs and other resources to enhance student learning (Borrego, 2006). A mapping process should identify both the formal elements of an institution's learning environment and the wide range of locations where informal learning also occurs. This step is a prerequisite to developing strategies for integrating the vast array of learning experiences that occur during college. Successful mapping of an institution's learning environment requires support and involvement at multiple levels of the organization. For example, senior leaders should advocate mapping and include it as part of the strategic planning process. Similarly, colleges and departments can develop learning maps for their units in collaboration with student affairs, food service, and other support services that shape the overall learning environment. At the micro level, individual professors and other education professionals can map their specific learning domain and how it can be integrated effectively into the larger educational community of their institution.

Once there is a clear and complete picture of where learning takes place in the college context, it is easier to identify opportunities to align learning activities, collaborate with colleagues to design complementary learning opportunities, and help students connect their learning in formal educational programs with learning that is occurring naturally in campus work settings, in residence halls, and the wide variety of out-of-class engagements that define much of the college experience.

Formal learning opportunities include all dimensions of the college curriculum such as courses and classroom learning, for-credit internships and practicums, study abroad programs, service learning, advising and counseling support, and supplemental instruction (e.g., academic peer tutoring). Identifying the full range of informal learning opportunities and venues is a more challenging, but equally important, task. As Borrego (2006) reports, learning occurs on athletic and debate teams, in campus housing, club activities and organizations, work-study jobs, student leadership activities, and peer mentoring. The full range of informal learning opportunities will vary with the mission, culture, and complexity of each higher education institution. The distinctive nature of individual colleges and universities is the reason each school must carefully examine the dimensions and attributes of its learning environment. Overlooking promising opportunities and experiences to complement and deepen students' learning would be easy without a detailed map of the varied places where college students learn both formally and informally.

Simple identification of locations for learning by itself is only part of the mapping process. Considering where natural or potential relationships exist to reinforce or extend learning is also important. In other words, where are the logical places to link learning that is occurring in isolation in order to expand understanding, test knowledge in context, and put theories and concepts into practice? Borrego (2006) explains that "successful learning happens in relationship—relations with new ideas, new people, and new ways of achieving" (p. 14). A strategic mapping process should identify places where learning alliances can be promoted to ensure that students' learning is adequately connected and mutually reinforcing. For example, how can out-of-class opportunities be identified for business majors where they can apply their marketing or accounting knowledge or how can opportunities for literature majors be created so that they can hone their skills as creative writers or future journalists? Forging links between the formal and informal learning that occurs in college can greatly enrich students' education by linking theory and principles learned in classes with practice in "on-the-job" or problem-solving settings. Integrated learning of this sort can also prepare students to use their education creatively when they leave college to enter the job market or contribute to their community as citizens.

Conditions Promoting Student Learning

A major synthesis of the research literature on how college affects students led to an explicit conclusion: students who are actively engaged in both academic and out-of-class activities gain more from the college experience than those who are not involved (Pascarella & Terenzini, 2005). Student engagement is influenced by two critical factors: what students do during college (e.g., the time and energy students devote to educationally purposeful activities) and what institutions do to facilitate learning and development (e.g., how an institution uses its resources to encourage students to participate in activities that lead to student success outcomes). Educators have only limited control over what students do, but they can help to create an educational environment with the type of structural features and pedagogical practices (Schneider, 2008) that foster and support student learning.

Promoting Deep and Transformative Learning. High-impact learning practices, when used effectively, can transform students' sense of themselves, understanding of the world, and ability to take command of their lives (Kuh, 2005). High-impact practices often provide students with different perspectives or alternative points of view that encourage students to question prior beliefs, understandings, or ways of doing things. According to transformative learning theory, "when people critically examine their habitual expectations, revise them, and act on the revised point of view, transformative learning occurs" (Cranton, 2006, p. 19); "transformative learning is a process of examining, questioning, validating, and revising our perspectives" (p. 23). Transformative learning occurs when people reconsider established frames of reference or understanding that no longer align with lived reality or do not seem as useful as they once were. When learners experience

NEW DIRECTIONS FOR HIGHER EDUCATION • DOI: 10.1002/he

this misalignment, they need to redefine their perspective on a problem or situation to make the perspective "more inclusive, discriminating, open, reflective" (Cranton, 2006, p. 36), and adaptable. Mezirow (2000) suggests that transformative learning enables adults to function more realistically and competently by helping them to integrate varied experiences more thoroughly and develop points of view that are broader and more discerning than unquestioned beliefs or habits of mind.

The authors of *Learning Reconsidered: A Campus-Wide Focus on the Student Experience* (National Association of Student Personnel Administrators [NASPA] & American College Personnel Association [ACPA], 2004) encouraged higher education to use all of its resources to educate and prepare students holistically. How best to use these resources to facilitate learning is a key question for all collegiate educators. In particular, what conditions promote the deep and transformational learning that are desirable outcomes of higher education? How do we promote the permanently embedded learning that alters and enhances a student's understanding of a subject in place of the surface learning that relies on memorization and is quickly lost once a course of other formal learning experience ends (Smith, MacGregor, Matthews, & Gabelnick, 2004)?

Drawing upon a constructivist paradigm, transformative learning theory explains that learning occurs when an individual encounters an alternative perspective and prior habits of mind or mental models are called into question (Cranton, 2006). This often can be an unplanned or haphazard process. Frequently, this disorganized and unintentional process is the case in educational settings where learners must integrate, with little guidance or support, what they learned in a formal setting, such as a classroom or a lab, with what they learned on the job, in a student leadership role, or through personal life experience. Alternatively, educators can be more intentional about helping students to link their varied learning experiences in order to enhance students' knowledge and understanding. When students are able to make the connections between the learning that occurs in the formal academic program and the informal learning that takes place throughout the college experience, then learning can become a comprehensive, holistic, and potentially transformative activity (NASPA & ACPA, 2004). To achieve this holistic learning, educators in and out of the classroom must be prepared to offer the type of guidance and support that encourages students to integrate their varied learning experiences and not leave this process to serendipity.

Two related strategies are instrumental in promoting deep and transformative learning. Mezirow (2003) claims that *discourse* helps to promote transformative learning. Structured and informal discussions and conversations assessing experiences, beliefs, feelings, and values among students and various members of the campus community can promote thoughtful reexamination of frames of reference and can lead learners to a more accurate and compelling understanding of the world one inhabits.

Similarly, careful *reflection* can help students to question long-held beliefs and unexamined assumptions in the light of new experiences and alternative viewpoints that may enrich their comprehension of complex issues (Brookfield, 2010).

Translating the concepts of discourse and reflection into effective education practice is a key task for educators. How can we use discourse and reflection to help students connect learning that occurs in varied settings but may be overlooked or segmented during the college years? How can we enrich an institution's learning environment by linking more strategically the formal curriculum with the natural, but informal, learning settings that engage students 24/7 in a process of meaning making, intellectual growth, and personal development? The integrated learning we advocate in this chapter lays the foundation for high-impact, and potentially transformative, learning. This type of connected learning encourages students to look at complex issues from multiple perspectives, connect formal and informal learning experiences, question assumptions that restrict understanding, and make new meaning that more accurately reflects a holistic view of reality. Cranton (2006) argues that transformative learning alters a person's self-perception, changes who a person is, and, ultimately, reshapes how a person engages with the world.

High-Impact Educational Practices.   An extensive body of literature has provided support for a set of 10 widely tested and used high-impact practices that provide substantial benefits to college students from an array of backgrounds (Kuh, 2008; Schneider, 2008). Although this literature includes decades of research, we briefly identify several HIPs and provide a few examples of ways educators might connect various components of the college experience with these practices. Readers interested in a more comprehensive and detailed description of these practices should refer to a number of publications by the Association of American Colleges and Universities such as: *High-Impact Educational Practices* (Kuh, 2008), *Five High-Impact Practices* (Brownell & Swaner, 2010), and *Ensuring Quality and Taking High-Impact Practices to Scale* (Kuh, O'Donnell, & Reed, 2013).

High-impact educational practices are tools educators can employ strategically to link diverse and often disjointed elements of the collegiate experience. Following are several examples that can provide opportunities to connect student learning.

First-year seminars and experiences are small seminar courses or other structured educational experiences designed to assist students in their transition to college. These first-year programs and experiences are designed to promote learning outcomes such as critical thinking, interpersonal and intrapersonal development, and practical competence. Discussions and writing assignments in first-year seminars can help new students adjust to college by focusing on transition issues like leaving home or living with a roommate. Similarly, first-year experiences that use common readings and discussion groups or encourage joint attendance at cultural events and

NEW DIRECTIONS FOR HIGHER EDUCATION • DOI: 10.1002/he

lectures can help new students get better acquainted with professors, advisers, and peers, helping them quickly develop a support network they can use to succeed in college.

Learning communities deliberately link selected college courses to encourage student interactions with peers and professors across these courses and beyond the classroom. Learning communities, with their intentional effort to connect learning in different settings, are an ideal place to consider how theories and concepts learned in classes compare with experiences in residence halls, jobs, and social settings. For example, a learning community that explores demographic diversity from the perspectives of sociology and economics could ask students to reflect on their observations of diversity issues on campus, in the local community, and from their own work history.

Writing intensive courses offered throughout the curriculum encourage students "to produce and revise various forms of writing for different audiences in different disciplines" (Kuh, 2008, p. 10). Writing is one key way to link the learning that occurs throughout the college environment because it provides an opportunity for active student reflection. Writing assignments drawing upon students' out-of-class experiences are a direct way to highlight the informal learning that occurs during college, encourage students to process this learning actively, and link it to the learning that occurs in the formal curriculum.

Undergraduate research can actively engage students from a wide variety of disciplines in all aspects of the empirical research process from learning how to ask research questions to making sense of results. Asking students to conduct research in their own collegiate environment is another way to connect the diverse forms of learning during college. Whether the focus is on topics such as economic inequity or environmental sustainability, research projects involving student peers, observing institutional systems, learning about grant management, or testing nearby lakes and streams, undergraduate research can break down barriers that segment learning during college and use out-of-class learning to illuminate the principles and theories covered in the formal curriculum. Action research projects focusing on current issues or problems in one's institution, community, or work setting may be a particularly effective way to integrate subject matter covered in academic programs with relevant learning opportunities elsewhere.

Diversity/global learning includes courses and programs where students are provided with opportunities to go beyond what is already familiar to them and explore cultures, life experiences, and worldviews different from their own. Courses on diversity, culture, and global issues can be sterile abstractions if they do not relate disciplinary theories and concepts to real-world experiences and problems. Educators can enrich the learning experience by encouraging students to reflect upon their study abroad trips or other off-campus learning experiences through the disciplinary lenses they are studying in courses. For example, the sociological concept of ethnocentrism becomes more meaningful if one considers how they have observed or been touched by an ethnocentric practice or policy.

Service learning/community-based learning involves students with community partners in direct experiences that offer students opportunities to apply knowledge from the curriculum in real-world settings. A key component of service/community learning is engaging in reflection and meaning-making from the experience (Kuh, 2005). Much service learning during college occurs as part of the service projects various types of student social, community, or religious organizations sponsor. Students may also have service learning experiences through volunteer work they do independent of their collegiate institution. Encouraging students to reflect upon these experiences can enhance the learning that results from helping students bridge their classroom and service learning experiences. Asking participants to consider their experience from the perspective of one's major or another disciplinary point of view (e.g., psychology, philosophy, anthropology, and business) is another way to integrate the collegiate learning experience and deepen understanding of a complex world.

Internships provide a direct work experience where professionals can provide students with supervision and socialization to a profession while encouraging students to integrate their classroom learning with knowledge acquired in a chosen field of work. Internships can be most beneficial when they give students concrete opportunities to apply and assess learning they have acquired in their college courses. Ideally, students have opportunities in classes or in meetings with advisers to develop their internship goals and later to process the internship experience in course papers or by assembling a portfolio. Thoughtful guidance and questioning from course instructors and advisers can help to make internships a valuable element of the college learning experience rather than an isolated work opportunity detached from the curriculum in the student's field of study.

Capstone courses and projects provide a culminating experience where students integrate and apply what they have learned in their varied collegiate experiences. Culminating experiences take many forms including senior theses, projects, comprehensive exams, and portfolios. What these experiences should have in common is a mechanism to encourage students to reflect on and make meaning of the many facets of their collegiate experience. Often culminating experiences limit their focus to the student's major field or the formal academic curriculum. In contrast, asking students to reflect on and integrate what they learned across the whole college experience can help a student understand what they gained during college, how they changed and developed, and what they have to offer employers and the larger society. Strategic questions or tasks can guide students through a systematic reflection and assessment process that can weave potentially fragmented learning experiences into a clearer and more meaningful tapestry as students complete the undergraduate years.

Responsibility for Linking Undergraduate Learning

Linking undergraduate learning is a shared, often collaborative, responsibility. Instructors, student affairs professionals, academic leaders, and students all have important parts to play in integrating the varied elements of the college learning environment. Instructors need to expand their focus beyond the boundaries of the individual courses they teach and take steps to link their classes to the larger educational mission of their institution and the goals of their individual students. Class activities and assignments that encourage students to relate their course topics to other subject fields and out-of-class learning opportunities can do much to help students develop well-integrated learning outcomes during college. Similarly, student affairs professionals can encourage students to apply principles and techniques from their courses in student organizations, leadership roles, and athletic activities.

Ideally, student affairs professionals and faculty members will collaborate on ways to complement each other's efforts to promote student learning and development. A strategic effort at Nelson Mandela Metropolitan University (NMMU) is an example of a collaborative academic affairs–student affairs strategy. In 2011, Nelson Mandela Metropolitan University (NMMU) in Port Elizabeth, South Africa, engaged in a campus-wide initiative to develop learning outcomes and map the cocurricular learning environment for its students (J. Winstead, personal communication, May 13, 2011). A committee of academic staff (i.e., faculty), student affairs administrators, and academic administrators developed a set of 16 learning goals for NMMU students. Although the initial focus was on the development of a cocurricular transcript, academic departments and programs have expressed considerable interest in linking classroom learning with specific and targeted cocurricular experiences for students (C. Foxcroft, personal communication, May 15, 2013). Student affairs educators are reviewing their programs and identifying the types of learning outcomes they can help to promote.

The 16 learning goals have established a common language between academic staff and student affairs staff, which has resulted in several benefits. First, student affairs staff can clearly articulate to campus constituents a set of desired outcomes for the various programs offered. Second, academic staff and senior administrators are aware of the types of outcomes students should expect from participation in the cocurricular experiences. Third, with the help of academic staff and student affairs administrators, students are encouraged to make connections between academic and cocurricular outcomes. Fourth, students are able to articulate learning outcomes from their collegiate experiences for potential employers or internship supervisors. The initiative at Nelson Mandela Metropolitan University is just

New Directions for Higher Education • DOI: 10.1002/he

one example of how those responsible for academic affairs and student affairs can collaborate and be intentional to help students link undergraduate learning.

Academic leaders, especially presidents and chief academic officers, also have an important role to play in efforts to better integrate collegiate learning. They need to articulate the importance of a well-integrated collegiate learning experience and advance this goal in their speeches and other communications with the institutional community. Central executive leaders need to spearhead any serious attempt to coordinate the segmented elements of an institution's learning environment. Without their moral and resource support, the vision of a well-integrated learning environment is unlikely to become reality. However, with leadership support, ambitious efforts to coordinate the collegiate learning environment, such as the strategy at NMMU, have great potential to transform an institution's educational climate.

Given the strong connection between student engagement and student learning and development, educators need to explain in multiple ways the importance of engagement and how students can seek out high-impact practices. For when students are engaged in HIPs, the odds increase for students investing time and effort in their education, interacting with faculty and peers around substantive issues, communicating with people different from themselves, receiving more frequent feedback from educators, and connecting abstract knowledge to practical experiences (Kinzie, 2011).

If higher education is going to engage college students in deep and transformative learning, it must use the existing research on high-impact learning to implement best practices with the potential to enhance the environment where students learn. Higher education must be more intentional in helping students to connect their varied experiences and the learning that occurs within them.

Cranton (2006) contends it is "our job as educators to come up with ways of creating that special moment when an individual thinks, 'Oh, wait, let me reconsider this one'" (p. 156). Essentially, this is what higher education is all about. This discovery process can happen by chance (as it too often does during the college years), or we can promote it by creating an educational environment that helps students connect, reflect on, assess, and make personal meaning of the multiple learning opportunities college offers. Our task is to help students take full advantage of these opportunities, integrate their varied learning experiences, and fulfill their potential as learners. This requires educators to think of learning more holistically and strategically than we usually do.

Educators should help students to examine and question their learning experiences critically through journaling, blogging, small group discussions, writing assignments, debates, role playing, and other analytical exercises designed to compare, contrast, and, ultimately, integrate the different dimensions of the college experience. A more holistic understanding of college combined with individual and collaborative efforts to tie learning together should help today's students to derive maximum benefit from the diverse learning opportunities higher education provides.

References

Association of American Colleges and Universities (AAC&U). (2007). *College learning for the new global century: A report from the National Leadership Council for Liberal Education and America's Promise.* Washington, DC: Author.

Barr, R. B., & Tagg, J. (1995). From teaching to learning: A new paradigm for undergraduate education. *Change, 27*(6), 12–25.

Borrego, S. (2006). Mapping the learning environment. In R. P. Keeling (Ed.), *Learning reconsidered 2: A practical guide to implementing a campus-wide focus on the student experience* (pp. 11–16). Washington, DC: ACPA, ACUHOI, ACUI, NACADA, NACA, NASPA, NIRSA.

Brookfield, S. (2010). Critical reflection as an adult learning process. In N. Lyons (Ed.), *Handbook of reflection and reflective inquiry* (pp. 215–236). New York, NY: Springer.

Brownell, J. E., & Swaner, L. E. (2010). *Five high-impact practices: Research on learning outcomes, completion, and quality.* Washington, DC: Association of American Colleges and Universities.

Chickering, A., & Gamson, Z. (1991). The seven principles for good practice in undergraduate education. In A. J. Chickering & Z. Gamson (Eds.), *New Directions for Teaching and Learning: No. 47. Applying the seven principles for good practice in undergraduate education* (pp. 63–69). San Francisco, CA: Jossey-Bass.

Cranton, P. (2006). *Professional development as transformative learning: New perspectives for teachers of adults.* San Francisco, CA: Jossey-Bass.

Keeling, R. P. (Ed.). (2006). *Learning reconsidered 2: A practical guide to implementing a campus-wide focus on the student experience.* Washington, DC: ACPA, ACUHOI, ACUI, NACADA, NACA, NASPA, NIRSA.

Kinzie, J. (2011, February). *Promoting high impact practices: Approaches to increase student engagement and access in the first year.* Paper presented at the Annual FYE Conference, Atlanta, GA.

Kuh, G. D. (2005). *Student success in college.* San Francisco, CA: Jossey-Bass.

Kuh, G. D. (2008). *High-impact educational practices: What they are, who has access to them, and why they matter.* Washington, DC: Association of American Colleges and Universities.

Kuh, G. D., O'Donnell, K., & Reed, S. (2013). *Ensuring quality and taking high-impact practices to scale.* Washington, DC: Association of American Colleges and Universities.

Mezirow, J. (2000). Learning to think like an adult. In J. Mezirow & Associates (Eds.), *Learning as transformation: Critical perspectives on a theory in progress* (pp. 3–33). San Francisco, CA: Jossey-Bass.

Mezirow, J. (2003). Transformative learning as discourse. *Journal of Transformative Education, 1*(1), 58–63.

National Association of Student Personnel Administrators (NASPA) & American College Personnel Association (ACPA). (2004). *Learning reconsidered: A campus-wide focus on the student experience.* Washington, DC: Author.

Pascarella, E. T., & Terenzini, P. T. (2005). *How college affects students: A third decade of research.* San Francisco, CA: Jossey-Bass.

Schneider, C. (2008). Introduction. In G. Kuh (Ed.), *High-impact educational practices: What they are, who has access to them, and why they matter* (pp. 1–8). Washington, DC: Association of American Colleges and Universities.

Smith, B. L., MacGregor, J., Matthews, R. S., & Gabelnick, F. (2004). *Learning communities: Reforming undergraduate education.* San Francisco, CA: Jossey-Bass.

MATTHEW WAWRZYNSKI is associate professor of educational administration and coordinator of the Higher, Adult, and Lifelong Education Program at Michigan State University.

ROGER BALDWIN is a professor of educational administration at Michigan State University.

NEW DIRECTIONS FOR HIGHER EDUCATION • DOI: 10.1002/he

6

Interprofessionalism involves learning from faculty members in different professions and is gaining popularity rapidly in health care. Every college campus has a wide variety of experts specifically educated in areas associated with good educational practices. This chapter describes the many ways in which faculty members from different professional areas may be supportive of one another.

Developing Learning in Faculty: Seeking Expert Assistance From Colleagues

Todd Zakrajsek

Graduate school provides a means for socialization regarding future roles of academics within a given content area via observation, discussion with program faculty members, and exploration of the literature (Austin, 2002). Yet, even after developing solid content expertise during graduate school, faculty members often enter new positions feeling ill prepared for their new roles as teachers (Gappa, Austin, & Trice, 2007; Rice, Sorcinelli, & Austin, 2000). One way to address this lack of preparation for effective teaching is the use of interprofessionalism as a means of support for developing faculty learning about how to be most successful as educators. Faculty members can learn from those on their own campus, but also from reading research by other faculty members on teaching and learning strategies.

Discipline-based scholarly work is an expected aspect of higher education and well supported within academe. However, expertise in a given content area is only one form of scholarship within higher education. For many years, a cohort of faculty in higher education have pushed and prodded institutions and faculty members to also become more scholarly with respect to teaching and assessment of student learning (Boyer, 1990; Hutchings & Shulman, 1999; Richlin, 2001). The goal remains to establish an expectation for all faculty to apply a scholarly approach to teaching and learning. According to this position, it seems natural to have the same care, nurturing, and study that pertain to disciplinary expertise also dedicated to teaching and student learning. Unfortunately, although attention is given to ensure individuals with terminal degrees are content experts, many new faculty members enter the classroom without specific training in teaching and learning (Gappa et al., 2007; Rice et al., 2000).

NEW DIRECTIONS FOR HIGHER EDUCATION, no. 165, Spring 2014 © 2014 Wiley Periodicals, Inc.
Published online in Wiley Online Library (wileyonlinelibrary.com) • DOI: 10.1002/he.20084

Even if you are a content expert, teaching is an extremely demanding profession. Consider the challenge of teaching 40 students in any course within any discipline. Aside from the content knowledge you have amassed, you need to possess the knowledge, skills, and abilities to effectively manage regular meetings of a fairly large number of individuals in a single room for several months. In very short order, many facets of scholarly teaching emerge: engaging an audience, facilitating group work, assessing written work, integrating new technologies, mediating disagreements, and giving feedback (often unpleasant feedback in the form of low grades).

The difficulty of taking a scholarly approach to teaching and learning lies in the challenge of being knowledgeable in multiple areas when necessary skills cross vastly different lines of professional content and often exhibit no similarity to your disciplinary expertise. The availability of solid information about effective teaching and learning continues to increase. Several examples will be provided in this chapter. In other cases, however, specialized information may best be learned by speaking with your colleagues. Faculty learning from one another and working across professional lines is an effective method to accomplish the wide variety of things expected of you when teaching a course, where both scholarly knowledge in your discipline and effective teaching are required.

One reason a college or university is such a special place is that it is teaming with exceptional talent in just about every content area imaginable. Yet, even with all of the expertise spread throughout the campus, most faculty members never consider colleagues as a resource to support their own teaching and learning. The good news is what when asked, colleagues are typically extremely pleased to be of assistance. Over the past 10 years, in practically every situation I thought of teaching and learning questions, I could find a colleague working within a short walk of my office who specialized in exactly the area in which I needed assistance. Often for the cost of a modest lunch or a cup of coffee, I could get some very helpful background, content knowledge, and advice for the challenges I faced. In one situation, I agreed to assist with the campus course management system. Very quickly I realized the hardware in place was grossly inadequate and proceeded immediately to secure new equipment. Unfortunately, it would take four to six weeks to receive and install what was needed. This became even more unfortunate because within a few days the system in place completely crashed. I faced the daunting task of telling faculty colleagues and students across campus that the system on which everyone relied, and for which I was responsible, was out of commission (without warning) for the remaining few weeks of the semester. As I pondered my next move, I suddenly thought about our communication department and that there must be an expert on "crisis communication." It took just a few quick phone calls to find a faculty member who specialized in delivering bad news. The assistance I received was not only very different from the message I had planned to deliver but was also right on target. With assistance from a discipline expert,

I was able to learn quickly how to address my professional need and maintain credibility with both faculty and students on campus.

Faculty Learning From Faculty—Interprofessional Topics

Included below are several specific skill areas that faculty members use to address common classroom issues. I provide examples of individuals who assisted me and who were outside my specific discipline area. These experiences underscore how interprofessional links are essential for faculty learning.

Providing Feedback.   Sitting down with a student or colleague and providing feedback is an essential component in a faculty member's academic life. Often the feedback contains information that is uncomfortable to deliver. Every time someone who has failed an exam, missed several classes, totally missed the mark on a term paper, is asked to "see me in my office," is given feedback on a presentation, or performed some task, a discussion with feedback is going to follow. Knowing what to say and how to say it is a critical aspect of your faculty life. Faculty in psychology can offer tips to other faculty members on how best to deliver feedback.

Providing the feedback in a developmental way is essential if the goal is to maintain motivation and to improve learning (Chism & Chism, 2007). Joe Lowman, an experienced clinical psychologist and author of a well-regarded book on teaching effectiveness (Lowman, 1995), proposes eight preparatory techniques for giving effective feedback following an observation of a faculty teaching:

1. Clarify the purpose of the observation.
2. Give the instructor choices about something.
3. Focus on seeing rather than evaluating behavior.
4. Encourage instructors to differentiate what they see from how they interpret the behavior.
5. Ask the instructor being observed to respond first.
6. Offer comments obliquely and tentatively.
7. Avoid a sense of undue seriousness.
8. Follow-up with instructors and faculty observers. (Lowman, in press)

Following these steps will greatly reduce your stress associated with giving feedback and also allow you to be much more productive in facilitating future progress, whether the feedback is given to an administrative assistant, a faculty member, or a student. In developing your skills as a faculty member and learning interprofessionally, it is encouraging to realize several individuals on campus have expert knowledge on how to deliver feedback in the most productive way possible.

Delivering Bad News—Crisis Communication.   Although rare, as a faculty member there are situations in which you will need to deliver bad news to a group of individuals (e.g., your class, department meeting, and alumni gathering). Delivering unpleasant news to a group or a class is particularly difficult. In addition to getting the point of the message across effectively, delivering information of a situation gone awry may cause harm to your reputation and result in a loss in confidence of your abilities in the future. The words you choose and action you take are both critically important.

How bad news is delivered has a substantial impact on how students will respond during class or perhaps the extent to which colleagues will look to you for assistance in the future. As noted above, much of your work as a faculty member in terms of both student learning and collegial interaction is based on your reputation as a professional. Work in the field of crisis management centers on the concept of reputational capital (Coombs, 2007; Fombrun & van Riel, 2004). Essentially, your total reputational capital contains the social and perceptual assets you hold. When you assist with a project and it goes well, you gain reputational capital. When you teach students a new concept and as a result they easily score well on an examination, you amass additional reputational capital. Bad news and mistakes, however, draw down your reputational capital.

Once, as an instructor I set up a review session on Sunday evening just prior to an important examination. Upon arriving at the building, which is a large building with multiple entrances, I found the building was unexpectedly locked. I lost some reputational capital that evening. In another case, one of the students in my class at a small college had died unexpectedly the evening before an exam. Some students in the class found out just minutes before the test was to start. I knew my words could either help or hurt the students in the course who were coming to grasp with this unexpected tragedy and also impact my reputational capital. In this case, I rescheduled the examination for later in the week. Some students were relieved, as they were in no frame of mind to take the exam. Others were upset as they had studied and planned to take the exam on that day. In the end, I was called to the Provost office and reprimanded for my action. Regardless of whether you agree with my decision or the position of the Provost, on that day I lost reputational capital with the Provost and some of the students, yet gained it with others. These examples illustrate that not all demands placed on you will have clear outcomes. The good news is that there are individuals specializing in this area on your campus who will gladly come to your aid.

Experts in crisis communication have many suggestions to help faculty members in other disciplines on campus. Seeger (2006) identified a helpful list of 10 best practices in crisis communication. Although most crisis communication is designed for organizations to address concerns of the public, application to the classroom and for faculty to address negative effects to students is readily apparent. Central components include preplanning; honest communication; sending messages that support self-efficacy; listening to, acknowledging, and expressing understanding of shared concerns; remaining accessible to answer questions; and accepting uncertainty and ambiguity (Seeger, 2006).

The one certainty about teaching is that things will not always go according to plan. When situations arise that have a negative impact on an entire class of students or committee of peers, seek out colleagues in the field of crisis communication for assistance. Individuals in departments of communication, public relations, or government often have a valuable understanding pertaining to scholarly work delivering bad news to groups.

Having Difficult Dialogues in the Classroom.   There are many situations in which it is expected that a discussion in a course will be challenging or difficult to mediate. It is your job as the faculty member for a course to push your students to the point that they are thinking in new and challenging ways.

It is typically best to not delve into any sensitive area using a class discussion model without thinking through how you will handle a heated discussion. Again, the good news is that there are many faculty members around with the exact information you need. For example, Sue, Torino, Capodilupo, Rivera, and Lin (2009) published the article "How White Faculty Perceive and React to Difficult Dialogues on Race: Implications for Education and Training." As noted just from the title, this scholarly work is directed at assisting with difficult discussions. Your campus may even have a faculty member leading a "difficult dialogue" initiative.

There are many important aspects to facilitating a challenging conversation. A few quick tips in this area include a caution to not focus completely on the words used and topic within the discussion itself, although that is certainly important. Equally important, and often neglected, is the need to consider the developmental level of the students in your course and extent to which you have built a feeling of community within the classroom (Center for Faculty Excellence, 2004).

Engaging in difficult conversations in class comes with responsibility, as conversations can easily erupt and result in an unproductive, or even psychologically harmful, shouting match. In thinking through who on campus may be able to provide some guidance on having difficult discussions in the classroom, think of areas in which difficult or challenging discussions are expected to happen on a regular basis. These areas include courses with a heavy emphasis on issues related to religion, politics, discrimination, and gender issues. Faculty members in departments focusing on these disciplinary areas deal with touchy topics regularly and frequently have delicate conversations in their courses. As a result, they have a variety of strategies pertaining to both how to moderate such discussions and how to support student learning.

Understanding How Students Learn and Work Together.   Psychologists study a host of behaviors that are important with respect to teaching and learning: motivation, group work, self-efficacy, learning, memory, and cognition. The work on human mindset is an area of research focused on determining ways to help students to be successful (Dweck, 2008). In a series of studies, Dweck (2008) found that students who perceive ability and intelligence as something that is "fixed" tend to not try as hard in novel situations. They believe one either has "it" (intelligence) or they don't. This has implications for your classroom as students who believe that those who study and work hard will succeed are much more likely to put extra effort than those who believe that some are naturally better at the requisite skill than others. To better understand mindset, your colleagues in the psychology department will likely be able to be of assistance.

Metacognition is another area with huge implications for student learning. Metacognition is a term that refers to essentially knowing the extent to which you know something. Your students may fail a test and indicate following the test that they "thought they knew the material better." On the other hand, you may clearly see situations when a student has "overprepared for the presentation" and neglected other areas of the course. Knowing when something is really known is important as it allows for allocating resources (such as time) effectively (Brinol & DeMarree, 2012).

Mindset and metacognition are just two concepts with serious implications for teaching and learning. Faculty members in the psychology department or education department on your campus are likely to be able to explain many areas of learning and motivation that will impact how you teach your students.

Assessing Student Learning.   One area in which I struggled early in my career was assessing student work. As an industrial psychologist, I was not specifically trained in grading term papers or oral presentations even though I did have training in developing employee evaluation systems. Professionals who may well have been specifically trained in evaluating written, oral, or performance work are likely found in areas such as English, communications, teacher education, theater, and music. The good news is that there are very solid frameworks for grading and assessing student work, and faculty in the areas noted above are exceptional in assessing the quality of work that many of us find difficult to grade. In an article by Dunbar, Brooks, and Kubicka-Miller (2006), three faculty members from communication departments teamed up to publish a performance-based rubric to assess communication skills. In this article, the authors demonstrated the value of the training process itself in better understanding the standards for evaluating oral presentations. They also note the importance of having communication departments assist in the assessment of communication skills throughout the university curriculum.

As an example of assessing written work, your English faculty colleagues will quickly point out that rubrics are valuable as they make explicit how the faculty member will grade the project, implicitly noting what the faculty member sees as important aspects of the project. Rubrics also provide specific feedback and allow students to better understand how to improve in the future. One of the most popular books on the topic was written by Walvoord and Anderson (2010). Jonsson and Svingby (2007) completed a review of the literature on grading rubrics and concluded that scoring reliability can be enhanced through the use of rubrics and that rubrics have the potential for promoting learning and improving instruction.

Assessing student learning can take a variety of forms. Group projects, oral presentations, term papers, and portfolios are just a few assignments that are fantastic learning opportunities, but may be difficult to assess accurately and in a reasonable amount of time. Again, as with the other skills noted in this chapter, the good news is that on your campus you likely have faculty colleagues who can be extremely helpful in this area.

Preparing Presentations: Visual Displays.   Interprofessional assistance possibilities span essentially every area of your professional life. In some situations, you may be assigning students the task of creating visual representations of content. In other situations, it may be you who is constructing the visual displays, such as a poster session presentation at a national conference in your discipline. For an upcoming conference or workshop, it may be beneficial to visit colleagues in the area of business, communication, or graphic design. Faculty members in these areas have been professionally trained in visual transmission of information. They would be particularly helpful in determining what makes an effective poster presentation, ways to enhance or enliven PowerPoint, and even specific expertise in designing grading rubrics if these activities are assigned to students.

MacIntosh-Murray (2007), a faculty member who teaches a course in "knowledge translation" in a health policy, management, and evaluation department, has published on the topic of the poster presentation as a specific method of communicating knowledge. In this publication, the author points out the subtle complexities involved in preparing and delivering an effective poster presentation. This article is not about font sizes and colors of graphic images, but rather the underlying meaning of the poster as a means to communicate. Understanding more about the role and meaning conveyed in a poster may be supported by tapping a faculty member teaching in the area of knowledge transmission. There are likely many faculty members on your campus trained in the area of visual communication and how to assess the effectiveness of the effort. In addition, marketing and art departments are also very helpful with respect to professional aspects of visual representation.

Student Support: Offices, Centers, and Programs

In addition to faculty members, there are wonderful resources throughout campus to assist you with a variety of issues pertaining to teaching and learning. The suggestion here is not that you take on the roles of these offices, but rather that you learn specific strategies from other professionals that you can incorporate into your courses. Also, many times knowing how the professionals on campus charged with assisting students actually assist students informs you on how to construct assignments in your course, how to write examinations, how to give feedback, or even the resources to which you can direct your students. It is amazing how long I taught at the university level before I really fully understood all of the resources available to my students.

Disability Student Services.   The office of Disability Student Services holds many opportunities to assist you with your teaching and creating effective learning opportunities for your students. This office has staff specifically dedicated to helping students learn in challenging situations. In amassing the expertise to directly work with students who struggle at the university, staff in this area learn a great deal about how people learn. Staff from this office can help you talk through how you teach your course. In every instance in which I have had such conversations, I have been given very concrete suggestions on how to teach my course even better.

Two areas of specific knowledge individuals in Disability Offices have are Universal Design for Instruction (UDI) and Universal Design for Learning (UDL). These areas look at ways to design education so that everyone has an opportunity to learn. In addition, thinking through UDI and UDL can be extremely helpful in curriculum design in general. For example, one principle of Universal Design for Instruction pertains specifically to feedback (Edyburn, 2010). According to UDI, it is ideal to design feedback to benefit all types of learners. This may include having students turn in parts of a large project at predetermined intervals rather than having the project all due at the end for a single grade. If there is a misunderstanding about the assignment or if a person has trouble with deadlines, the student may well fail the course entirely because of a final deadline. Other UDI principles include consideration for class climate, interaction among students and with the instructor, delivery methods, and assessment (as differentiated from feedback). Many faculty have used principles of Universal Design, and it is poised to have a large impact on education in the future (Edyburn, 2010).

At times, interprofessional collaborations with student support offices lead to new resources. Langford-Von Glahn, Zakrajsek, and Pletcher-Rood (2008) teamed up to provide tips for assisting students with Asperger's syndrome in the classroom. Langford-Von Glahn and Zakrajsek are both psychologists and Pletcher-Rood works in a Developmental Disability Office. These authors point out that many of the provisions that may be made for students with Asperger's syndrome (as well as other disabilities) may well be beneficial for all students. Discussions with your office of Disability Student Services may well shed a light on many potential instructional improvements you may be able to make in your courses with very little effort.

Student Success Center.   The Student Success Center (a.k.a. Academic Success Center or Tutoring Center) helps students who are struggling academically. Those offices typically have tremendous resources for both you and your students as they are designed to help students better understand how they learn, suggest ways to take good notes during class, provide study tips for exams, and even how to think like an engineer (or insert any discipline). The items listed in the previous sentence, and so many other services offered in these offices, are all areas that may inform how you teach or design your curriculum. For example, in setting up a review session for an upcoming examination, meeting quickly with the academic success center may well provide you with some tips you can give your students pertaining to studying for the exam. Meeting with a staff member from this center may also provide very easy to implement suggestions you can pass on to your students about how to better take notes, which will also assist you in the pacing at which you deliver content.

Writing Center.   I have long thought it should be a requirement for all new faculty members to speak with someone in the Writing Center within the first 90 days on campus. The staff of this office knows exactly where students struggle with respect to writing. If you know those areas prior to creating your assignments, you will know ahead of time where your students will face difficulty. Writing Center staff members have also been very helpful to me in designing grading rubrics for my assignments. Every time I have done this I have made positive changes in my assignment and my rubric. Keep in mind that one of the best ways to increase student learning and to decrease your time spent grading is to have the students write really good papers. Improved student writing can be facilitated by ensuring that your assignments are designed well and that there is a good grading mechanism in place. Writing Center staff are excellent at assisting in both of these areas.

Center for Teaching and Learning.   If your campus has a Center for Faculty Development, you have another area in which you can gain invaluable assistance. Individuals in such centers often specialize in areas that can be of great assistance to you. Increasingly, centers of faculty support offer resources in leadership and scholarly activity. Whenever you are frustrated by something or find a task difficult, it is valuable to make a quick call to this office. They will not be able to remove all the hassles from your job, but they will likely know ways to ease your burden and facilitate better learning for your students. In addition, if they are unable to help you directly, they will likely be able to tell you who can be of assistance. These centers typically have the name "Center for Teaching and Learning," "Faculty Center for Innovative Teaching," "Center for Excellence in Teaching and Learning," or in medical schools something akin to "Academy of Educators."

Conclusion

A level of expertise based on disciplinary knowledge should be expected from every person who teaches a course. Likewise, a scholarly understanding of teaching and learning should also be present. Unfortunately, it is next to impossible for you to be an expert in the wide variety of areas needed to effectively facilitate student learning. Luckily, there are individuals throughout the campus who have very specific training in essentially every area needed by essentially every faculty member. The first step in securing assistance interprofessionally is to recognize when information is needed; the second step is to locate the person on campus who can provide the information you need. If you are not certain where to find such individuals, first speak with a senior member of your department who may be willing to assist you, such as your mentor (by the way, if you do not have a mentor it is wise to find one). Another option to secure assistance from colleagues in other professions is to call a department where you suspect someone with the specific content expertise you seek is employed and ask the office professional for suggestions. Finally, there are times it is best to walk over to a department and have an informal conversation with whomever you can catch in the hall. Explain which department you are from and why you are seeking assistance. In several decades of teaching I have been approached in this way by only a few faculty members, and in each case I was extremely happy to be of assistance to my colleagues.

Of course, in addition to speaking with individuals on your campus, there is a great deal of scholarly work published in a variety of skill areas needed by faculty members. Much of this work is written for interdisciplinary audiences and therefore at a level that is relatively easy to read. A good number of the skills needed to be a solid faculty member are also of interest to the general public. As a result, many of the tips and techniques needed for things such as creating a good visual representation, components of a good speech, and managing groups can be found in published work written for a lay audience.

Taking an interprofessional approach to improving the design, delivery, and assessment of student learning is also likely to have a fantastic side benefit in that when something is done well it typically takes less of your time and energy. Investing a small amount of time in getting expert advice from colleagues typically will likely have a very quick return on that initial investment. Of course, it is also a great way to make good friends across campus. In the process of building your interprofessional network on campus, you may well find yourself to be one of the most valuable people on faculty as you will know where on campus all of the talent lies when it comes to good teaching and effective student learning.

References

Austin, A. E. (2002). Preparing the next generation of faculty: Graduate school as socialization to the academic career. *Journal of Higher Education, 73*, 94–122.

Boyer, E. (1990). *Scholarship reconsidered: Priorities of the professoriate* (Vol. 147). Menlo Park, CA: The Carnegie Foundation for the Advancement of Teaching.

Brinol, P., & DeMarree, K. G. (2012). *Social metacognition*. New York, NY: Taylor and Francis.

Center for Faculty Excellence. (2004). *Teaching controversial issues.* Retrieved from http://cfe.unc.edu/pdfs/FYC21.pdf

Chism, N. V. N., & Chism, G. (2007). *Peer review of teaching: A sourcebook* (2nd ed.). Boston, MA: Anker Publishing.

Coombs, T. W. (2007). Protecting organization reputations during a crisis: The development and application of situational crisis communication theory. *Corporate Reputation Review, 10*, 163–176.

Dunbar, N. E., Brooks, C. F., & Kubicka-Miller, T. (2006). Oral communication skills in higher education: Using a performance-based evaluation rubric to assess communication skills. *Innovative Higher Education, 31*(2), 115–128.

Dweck, C. (2008). *Mindset the new psychology of success: How you can fulfill your potential.* New York, NY: Ballantine Books.

Edyburn, D. L. (2010). Would you recognize Universal Design for Learning if you saw it? Ten propositions for new directions in the second decade of UDL. *Learning Disability Quarterly, 33*(1), 33–41.

Fombrun, C. J., & van Riel, C. B. M. (2004). *Fame & fortune: How successful companies build winning reputations.* New York, NY: Prentice-Hall Financial Times.

Gappa, J. M., Austin, A. A., & Trice, A. G. (2007). *Rethinking faculty work: Higher education's strategic imperative.* San Francisco, CA: Jossey-Bass.

Hutchings, P., & Shulman, L. S. (1999). The scholarship of teaching: New elaborations, new developments. *Change, 31*(5), 10–15.

Jonsson, A., & Svingby, G. (2007). The use of scoring rubrics: Reliability, validity, and educational consequences. *Educational Research Review, 2*, 130–144.

Langford-Von Glahn, S. J., Zakrajsek, T. D., & Pletcher-Rood, S. (2008). Teaching students with Asperger syndrome (and other disabilities) in the college classroom: Creating an inclusive learning environment. *Journal of Excellence in College Teaching, 19*(2–3), 107–133.

Lowman, J. (1995). *Mastering the techniques of teaching* (2nd ed.). San Francisco, CA: Jossey-Bass.

Lowman, J. (in press). Preparing faculty to teach from a developmental perspective. *Journal of Faculty Development, 28*(2).

MacIntosh-Murray, A. (2007). Poster presentations as a genre in knowledge communication: A case study of forms, norms and values. *Science Communication, 28*(3), 347–376.

Rice, R. E., Sorcinelli, M. D., & Austin, A. E. (2000). *Heeding new voices: Academic careers for a new generation.* New Pathways Inquiry No. 7. Washington, DC: American Association for Higher Education.

Richlin, L. (2001). Scholarly teaching and the scholarship of teaching. In C. Kreber (Ed.), *Scholarship revisited: Perspectives on the scholarship of teaching and learning* (pp. 57–68). San Francisco, CA: Jossey-Bass.

Seeger, M. W. (2006). Best practices in crisis communication: An expert panel process. *Journal of Applied Communication Research, 34*(3), 232–244.

Sue, D. W., Torino, G. C., Capodilupo, C. M., Rivera, D. P., & Lin, A. I. (2009). How White faculty perceive and react to difficult dialogues on race: Implications for education and training. *The Counseling Psychologist, 37*(8), 1090–1115.

Walvoord, B. E., & Anderson, V. J. (2010). *Effective grading: A tool for learning and assessment in college.* San Francisco, CA: Jossey-Bass.

TODD ZAKRAJSEK *is an associate professor and associate director of fellowship programs in the Department of Family Medicine and the executive director of the Academy of Educators in the School of Medicine at the University of North Carolina at Chapel Hill.*

NEW DIRECTIONS FOR HIGHER EDUCATION • DOI: 10.1002/he

*This chapter reviews institutional approaches to blended learning
and the ways in which institutions support faculty in the
intentional redesign of courses to produce optimal learning. The
chapter positions blended learning as a strategic opportunity to
engage in organizational learning.*

7

Blended Learning as Transformational Institutional Learning

Kim VanDerLinden

Blended learning is broadly defined as replacing seat time in courses with
online activities to achieve learning objectives. Garrison and Vaughan
(2008) argue that blended learning is "the thoughtful fusion of face-to-
face and online learning experiences" (p. 5) such that the strengths of each
mode are blended into an optimal learning experience. At most institutions,
a blended course is synonymous with a hybrid course. Whether termed hybrid or blended, a key feature of this mode of instruction is that it requires
a fundamental course redesign that transforms the structure and approach
to student learning (Garrison & Vaughan, 2008).

Blended learning exists on a continuum with minimal online activities
on one end and minimal face-to-face activities on the other end. Most institutions do not prescribe a definition of blended learning and acknowledge
that it has different meanings for different disciplines and can fall anywhere
in the continuum. When colleges and universities fail to define blended
learning at an institutional level, however, it is then reduced to the broadest
understanding and open to interpretation regarding the ratio of face-to-face
time and online interaction and activities. The absence of a precise definition undermines the important distinctions made by Garrison and Vaughan
(2008) that blended learning is a transformational redesign of teaching and
learning. And the broad definition then lends itself to blended learning becoming a mere description of a singular course rather than an institutional
strategy. For example, a course may require significant online interaction
between students and faculty through discussion boards and other online
mechanisms; however, this course may not have the label of blended due
to the fact that it still meets the typical three hours a week. Alternatively,
a course may be labeled as a blended learning course simply because an

instructor is effectively transferring course content into the Learning Management System (LMS) and meeting two times a week instead of three. Viewing courses on a case-by-case basis and applying the label of blended based on a nebulous definition limits the opportunity to position blended learning as an institutional strategy.

Examples abound of single courses being transformed through the incorporation of online activities. Glazer (2011), for example, edited a volume of articles on blended learning in several different disciplines. And Shank (2007) published 95 examples of ways to enhance technology-based and blended learning courses. But consider the following quote from an instructor in culinary arts:

> I wish I could say that as I moved into the realm of blended learning I carefully considered the associated educational issues and took a grounded research approach; however, the reality was it was more a matter of looking at my resources and abilities and selecting tasks that were achievable. (Behnke, 2011, p. 15)

Imagine how this quote may have been different if this instructor was first provided with a clear definition of blended learning for his institution, as well as provided with an understanding of the institutional approach and support mechanisms to create a transformational redesign of this course. Just as the curriculum can become a collection of courses instead of a cohesive and meaningful curriculum, the same may be true for blended learning when the approach does not provide the mechanisms and support to fundamentally redesign the student learning experience across the curriculum.

According to Glazer (2011), a challenge of blended learning is effectively linking the two mediums (face-to-face and online) so that the two reinforce each other and create a single, unified course. Yet, prior to addressing this microlevel challenge, another macrolevel challenge exists; namely, how does an institution create a unified approach to blended learning that is then instilled in individual courses to create a cohesive and meaningful approach to transforming student learning?

Strategic Approaches to Blended Learning

Taking a strategic approach to blended learning requires an understanding of what a strategy is versus an initiative or goal. The term strategy is commonplace in higher education, but sometimes the definition of strategy is forgotten as constituents go about their daily tasks. Strategy clarifies purposes and priorities, mobilizes motivation and resources, and sets directions for the future (Morrill, 2007). Institutions use strategy to deal with changing environments and strategic decisions affect the overall welfare of the organization (Chaffee, 1985). A strategic approach to blended learning is not prescriptive, nor is it a fixed plan. Rather, a strategic approach provides an overarching plan framed by the leadership with clear support structures (Rowley & Sherman, 2001). Faculty and instructional designers are still the experts executing the strategy for blended learning, but this approach allows for a transformational view of learning as courses are intentionally redesigned with appropriate support structures.

A hoped-for outcome of blended learning is that students may experience transformational learning experiences (Cranton, 2006). Taking a strategic approach to blended learning also has the potential to create transformational organizational learning opportunities as faculty, instructional designers, and administrative leaders engage in critical reflection about the redesign of courses to achieve optimal learning (Kezar, 2013). Transformational learning for an individual is a process of critical reflection whereby an individual has a change in their frame of reference (Mezirow, 1997). Transformational learning at the organizational level can be conceptualized as a process whereby the institution makes a significant shift in the frame of reference around institutional strategies and initiatives. Organizational learning is not the simple sum of the learning of its members. Rather, some learning is embedded in the systems, structures, routines, practices, and strategies (Crossan, Lane, & White, 1999). The process of creating blended learning opportunities presents the institution with the chance to shift the frame of reference from individual faculty creating individual courses to the institution embarking on the execution of a learning strategy that expands well beyond individual courses.

Researchers at Brigham Young University (Graham, Woodfield, & Harrison, 2013) studied the stages that institutions go through when adopting blended learning. The stages include awareness/exploration, adoption/early implementation, and mature implementation/growth. In the awareness stage, no institutional strategies exist, but there is an institutional awareness and there might be individual faculty members who are being supported in their efforts. In the adoption phase, new policies and practices are implemented to support blended learning. And in the mature stage, well-established strategies, structures, and support mechanisms exist for blended learning. If these stages sound familiar, it is because similar stages are typically found in other studies of organizational change (see Kezar, 2001, for a review of organizational change theories in higher education). Some may be familiar with the stages of change that begin with mobilization (providing vision and harnessing enthusiasm), move to implementation (ensuring appropriate structures and processes are in place), and then become institutionalized (measuring progress and ensuring continuous growth; Kezar, 2009), which mirror the stages laid out by Graham and colleagues (2013).

If the adoption of blended learning follows the typical trajectory of organizational change, what is unique about the adoption of blended learning as an organizational strategy? The pressures on higher education in 2014 are perhaps greater than in any other time period. The strategic adoption of blended learning is interconnected to all the issues that are front of mind for decision makers such as accessibility, affordability, limited resources, and competition, not to mention perhaps the greatest interconnected concern—student learning. Competition for students is fierce as more and more alternatives to traditional higher education come into the fold. And outside entities offering variations on blended learning are seen as threats to higher education as the dubbed "year of the MOOC" in 2012 caused many in higher education to ponder whether lecture halls will soon be extinct (Kvan, 2013; Palmer, 2012). In August of 2013, even President Barack Obama made it clear that higher education needs to change. During a speech focused on college affordability, he articulated the need to "jumpstart new competition between colleges … in terms of innovation that encourages affordability, and encourages student success, and doesn't sacrifice educational quality" (The White House, Office of the Press Secretary, 2013, para. 46). While the President could have left this vague statement hanging, he went on to cite specific examples:

> Universities like Carnegie Mellon and Arizona State, they're starting to show that online learning can help students master the same material in less time and often at lower cost. Georgia Tech, which is a national leader in computer science, just announced it will begin offering an online master's degree in computer science at a fraction of the cost of a traditional class, but it's just as rigorous and it's producing engineers who are just as good. (The White House, Office of the Press Secretary, 2013, para. 64)

Given the current challenges and demands on institutions, it is hard to imagine a college or university that can afford to *not* take a strategic approach to blended learning.

The Role of Technology.   As we step back and consider the broader impact of technology in the current context of higher education, Amara's Law seems particularly applicable. Roy Amara was a past president of the Institute for the Future, a think tank established in the 1960s, and his law states that we tend to overestimate the effect of a technology in the short run and underestimate the effect in the long run. And because we have potentially overestimated the short-term effect of technology integration, stakeholders are looking for immediate and significant outcomes. Amara's Law may also explain some of the skepticism from faculty colleagues (Inside Higher Education, 2013). The hype is huge, but constituents are not viewing blended learning as a long-term strategy.

The overestimation of the effect of technology also results in an environment where faculty members may not be comfortable taking risks in the redesign of their courses. Instead, faculty may be questioning how far to take a course redesign knowing that the outcomes will be carefully scrutinized and compared to the traditional face-to-face course outcomes. Fear of scrutinized outcomes may only be a minor concern for faculty and the larger concerns may relate to the lack of time, support, or incentives. Over the past 20 years, faculty developers have noted that a major institutional need is training faculty to integrate technology into their classroom teaching (Sorcinelli, Austin, Eddy, & Beach, 2006). A well-thought-out institutional strategy for blended learning not only alleviates some of the concerns and challenges for faculty but it also provides a long-term plan that does not overestimate the effects and outcomes in the short term.

The Role of Faculty.   Dee Fink (2013) writes of significant, deep learning experiences and provides a framework for situating blended learning as an opportunity for transformational organizational learning. A first critical condition is to become aware that a better way exists. Faculty members need to become aware of their own need to learn and change (Fink, 2013). Transferring this idea to blended learning, a first step is to allow stakeholders to see that a better way exists to produce optimal learning in courses. As more and more research on the effectiveness of blended learning becomes available, it becomes easier to show campus constituents the evidence that there is a better way to produce optimal learning.

Sharing the following statement can result in the first step toward transformational learning experiences for campus members: blended learning can result in significantly better learning than in a traditional classroom (Glazer, 2011; U.S. Department of Education, 2009; Zhao, Lei, Yan, Lai, & Tan, 2005). In the current learning context in which showing the evidence of student learning is perhaps one of the highest priorities facing institutions, this statement bears repeating—*blended learning can result in significantly better learning than in a traditional classroom.* Two studies reviewed and summarized by Glazer (2011) include a meta-analysis of the U.S. Department of Education in 2009, and a study by Zhao and colleagues in 2005. The studies conclude that students in blended learning courses performed significantly better than students in completely online courses or students in face-to-face courses. As Glazer (2011) explains, however, it is entirely inappropriate to assume then that all online learning is superior regardless of how it is implemented. In fact, the research points clearly to the idea that it is the implementation, the pedagogy (particularly the active learning strategies), and the design of courses that result in better learning.

The research about the effectiveness of blended learning provides a powerful jolt for campus members. Of note, a recent Inside Higher Education (2013) survey of faculty attitudes toward technology found large amounts of skepticism among faculty members about the quality of online learning. This finding of high levels of skepticism, taken out of context, raises more questions than answers. What specifically are faculty members skeptical about—the learning outcomes, the pedagogical approaches, and student engagement in online activities? And if faculty members are the instructional designers in most instances, does that mean they are skeptical about their own work as novices or the work of their colleagues? The results become clearer when we keep in mind that most faculty members who were surveyed do not actually teach online. Moreover, the survey revealed that appreciation of the quality of online courses grows with instructors' experiences teaching online. In order to achieve Fink's condition of awareness, it seems necessary to expose and deconstruct this skepticism, perhaps debunking some of the myths while also affirming some of the skepticism through defining what blended learning is and is not. Faculty members need encouragement from others and they need to "celebrate one another's success in trying something new" (Fink, 2013, p. 222). And as the Inside Higher Education survey findings suggest, faculty members who are already engaged in blended learning are critical players in creating awareness, encouraging others, and celebrating success.

Another insight into Fink's (2013) overview of creating significant learning experiences is that they need to be built into the curriculum, not just into individual courses. As mentioned above, examples of blended learning strategies for singular courses abound. In fact, in an analysis of over 200 theses and dissertations on blended learning, Drysdale, Graham, Spring, and Halverson (2013) classified 83% of the studies as being focused on the course level. Less than 1% of the studies were classified as having an institutional focus. Even though the examples of an institutional approach to blended learning are scarce, presenting best practices for blended learning only in the context of individual courses prevents constituents from grasping the larger institutional strategy. Situating all specific course examples within the framework of the larger institutional strategy allows the rationale for blended learning to remain at the forefront of the conversations, as well as at the forefront of any specific processes and support mechanisms the institution puts into place. Delving into specific course strategies should always be preceded by reminding constituents of the larger institutional strategy.

The Role of Institutions.   Researchers and scholars consistently stress the importance of providing institutional support in order to achieve a strategy, to change the culture, or to achieve organizational learning (Fink, 2013; Kezar, 2009; Rowley & Sherman, 2001). Institutions need to ensure that they are providing the necessary training on successful blended learning pedagogical approaches. Team-based learning, problem-based learning, and other successful pedagogical approaches may be regular professional development topics, but even at institutions that have achieved the more mature stage of implementation, seldom are professional development opportunities solely focused on team-based learning in blended learning courses. And if courses are offered, they may be offered out of the mainstream and positioned as a chance to learn about using technology rather than presented as an institutional approach to redesigning pedagogy.

When creating the needed support structures, time is an important consideration. Glazer (2011) stated that "one of the unexpected benefits of blended learning is that it has the effect of creating time" (p. 4). The author, however, seems to only be referring to the student perspective rather than the faculty or a larger institutional perspective. For students, Glazer concludes that the time spent online is already excessive and that blended learning may not even feel like they are doing course work. Rather, being online is a way of life for students. In contrast, the National Science Foundation Task Force on Cyberlearning (2008) stated that today's students use computers, phones, and other devices for almost every form of communication *except* learning.

Students' comfort level online does not make up for the fact that faculty need time to become equally comfortable and to create optimal learning opportunities for students. A perceived downside of blended learning may be the lack of time to effectively redesign courses, particularly as the institution is moving along the stages from awareness and exploration to adoption and mature implementation. Fink (2013) notes that the prevailing view of faculty work (teaching, research, and service) does not provide any "in-load" time for faculty to work on their own professional development around teaching (p. 222). Therefore, a critical condition necessary for the achievement of a blended learning institutional strategy is adequate time.

Blended Learning at Northern Arizona University

Northern Arizona University (NAU) has long been proactive, rather than reactive, when it comes to technology integration. NAU entered the realm of distance learning close to 40 years ago. For NAU, blended learning is positioned as an initiative within a larger strategy related to educational excellence. Specifically, the NAU strategic plan states that a key strategy that expands access to higher education and improves student learning is the redesign of curricular protocols while incorporating technology (Northern Arizona University, 2013). Many institutions are similar to NAU in that blended learning is a strategic imperative.

Also, like many institutions, student learning at NAU is certainly at the forefront of the blended learning strategy, but there is also the growing competition from completely online programs and the internal and external pressure to keep up, to not lose ground, and to thrive through institutional efficiencies. These pressures demand short-term solutions, but as discussed above, overestimating the short-term effects will likely lead to disappointing outcomes. Therefore, NAU is taking several steps to ensure long-term benefits through the institutionalization of blended learning, rather than quick fix implementations on a course-by-course basis.

Prior to 2013, the growth of blended learning at NAU was largely due to individual faculty member adoption and the President's Technology Initiative. Support for NAU faculty is an important element in NAU's strategic approach and illuminates the importance of creating a new reward system to foster and support change (Rowley & Sherman, 2001). The President's Technology Initiative pairs faculty members with e-Learning Center instructional designers and offers faculty two important things: an incentive and the time to redesign a course. The goals of the initiative are to serve more students at a lower cost per student, to reduce the number of in-person classes while increasing structured out-of-class learning activities, to focus on innovative course design that emphasizes higher order learning, and to cement NAU's reputation as a leader in student success and the use of technology.

While originally championed by the president and the NAU e-Learning Center, the blended learning initiative shifted to the Provost's Office in 2013. This move clearly situated blended learning in the larger context of student learning at NAU, rather than as a technology initiative. And explicit evidence of NAU's strategic approach to blended learning is the creation of a full-time position in the Provost's Office to oversee progress toward the implementation of blended learning and to serve as what Rowley and Sherman (2001) refer to as the "change champion" (p. 173). Denise Helm (personal communication, September 4, 2013), a former associate dean of the College of Health and Human Services at NAU and an American Council on Education (ACE) Fellow, assumed the position in 2013 and has already seen a cultural shift related to blended learning. Due to her efforts and the creation of a Blended Learning Leadership Team, a shared and clear definition of blended learning at NAU is emerging. A blended learning web page is set to launch and will feature the definition, as well as additional resources. In addition, Helm, along with the director of the e-Learning Center, Don Carter, is meeting with the administrative teams of each of the academic Colleges to identify courses that are primed for a blended learning course redesign. And she also plans to survey faculty about their attitudes and behaviors related to blended learning to identify the structural barriers facing faculty.

Once barriers are identified, Helm in partnership with the Faculty Development Office will take specific steps to support faculty and staff through professional development initiatives. According to Larry Gallagher (personal communication, August 29, 2013), NAU's Director of Faculty Development, blended learning requires intentional and transformational thinking about student learning. Gallagher views the adoption of blended learning from a technological innovation perspective when he states that "the perceived pain of change, in this case the change from traditional face-to-face to blended learning, must be less than the perceived pain of staying the same." And in his efforts in providing faculty professional development, he is focused on the creation of a critical mass of faculty and key individuals to take blended learning from an initiative to a strategy. For example, the Faculty Professional Development Office created a learning community focused specifically on blended learning course redesign. And in the next academic year, new faculty orientation and associated efforts will utilize a blended learning approach offering new faculty the opportunity to experience blended learning firsthand.

NEW DIRECTIONS FOR HIGHER EDUCATION • DOI: 10.1002/he

NAU has transformed blended learning from being a technology initiative situated on the periphery of the institution to a strategy that is at the epicenter of student learning. While focused on long-term gains, with the creation of a dedicated position out of the Provost's Office, NAU has experienced noticeable shifts in the culture as constituents are focused on intentionally redesigning courses to enhance student learning.

Blended Learning as a Strategy

The implementation of blended learning at colleges and universities needs to be positioned as an institutional strategy that can result in organizational learning. Garrison and Vaughan (2013) concluded that blended learning has not resulted in organizational change that significantly enhances the effectiveness of the teaching and learning transaction and suggest that institutions need to engage in critical self-reflection about the learning experience. The responsibility of redesigning learning in blended learning courses falls squarely on faculty and instructors. The responsibility of positioning blended learning as an institutional strategy falls squarely on the leadership. Institutional leaders have the opportunity to provide structures and support that allow instructors to transform their courses.

The following list of questions may assist in institutional efforts to approach blended learning as a strategy rather than as a label in the course catalog:

- Has your institution provided a definition of blended learning that is widely known and disseminated?
- What is the rationale for blended learning at your institution? Is the rationale clear and included in the definition? Why is blended learning a priority at your institution?
- Is the rationale for blended learning and message framed consistently by leadership, administrators, and faculty—from the president to instructional designers to department chairs?
- What processes, structures, and support exist at the institution for blended learning? Who is the "change champion" for blended learning?
- What success stories exist in single courses and how does that success translate to institutional success?
- How will the institution know when blended learning is working—not just on a course-by-course basis but as an institution? How will the institution assess the impact of blended learning on the institution?

Answers to these questions have the potential to clarify the institutional approach to blended learning beyond what may be happening in individual courses. When done well, blended learning combines the best attributes of face-to-face and online learning (Glazer, 2011). While true for singular courses, much more is required for institutions to be perceived as doing blended learning well. When done well at the institutional level, blended learning implementation is guided by a clear strategy that allows constituents to engage in organizational learning while redesigning and transforming courses for optimal learning.

References

Behnke, C. (2011). Blended learning in the culinary arts: Tradition meets technology. In F. Glazer (Ed.), *New pedagogies and practices for teaching in higher education: Blended learning: Across the disciplines, across the academy* (pp. 13–30). Sterling, VA: Stylus.

Chaffee, E. (1985). Three models of strategy. *Academy of Management Review, 10*(1), 89–98.

Cranton, P. (2006). *Professional development as transformative learning: New perspectives for teachers of adults.* San Francisco, CA: Jossey-Bass.

Crossan, M., Lane, H., & White, R. (1999). An organizational learning framework: From intuition to institution. *Academy of Management Review, 24*(3), 522–537.

Drysdale, J., Graham, C., Spring, K., & Halverson, L. (2013). An analysis of research trends in dissertations and theses studying blended learning. *Internet and Higher Education, 17,* 90–100.

Fink, L. D. (2013). *Creating significant learning experiences: An integrated approach to designing college courses, revised and updated.* San Francisco, CA: Jossey-Bass.

Garrison, D., & Vaughan, N. (2008). *Blended learning in higher education.* San Francisco, CA: Jossey-Bass.

Garrison, D., & Vaughan, N. (2013). Institutional change and leadership associated with blended learning innovation: Two case studies. *Internet and Higher Education, 18,* 24–28.

Glazer, F. (2011). *New pedagogies and practices for teaching in higher education: Blended learning: Across the disciplines, across the academy.* Sterling, VA: Stylus.

Graham, C., Woodfield, W., & Harrison, J. (2013). A framework for institutional adoption and implementation of blended learning in higher education. *Internet and Higher Education, 18,* 4–14.

Inside Higher Education. (2013). *The 2013 survey of faculty attitudes towards technology.* Retrieved from http://www.insidehighered.com/audio/2013/09/12/2013-survey-faculty-attitudes-technology

Kezar, A. (2001). *Understanding and facilitating organizational change in the 21st century: Recent research and conceptualizations.* Washington, DC: ASHE-ERIC Higher Education Report.

Kezar, A. (2009, January). *Synthesis of scholarship on change in higher education.* Paper presented at Mobilizing STEM Education for a Sustainable Future, Emory University, Atlanta, GA.

Kezar, A. (2013). *How colleges change: Understanding, leading, and enacting change.* New York, NY: Routledge.

Kvan, T. (2013, July 13). Why the MOOC cannot trump the campus. *University World News.* Retrieved from http://www.universityworldnews.com/article.php?story=20130712103200884

Mezirow, J. (1997). Transformative learning: Theory to practice. In P. Cranton (Ed.), *New Directions for Adult and Continuing Education: No. 74. Higher education: A global community* (pp. 5–12). San Francisco, CA: Jossey-Bass.

Morrill, R. (2007). *Strategic leadership: Integrating strategy and leadership in colleges and universities.* Westwood, CT: Greenwood Publishing Group.

National Science Foundation Task Force on Cyberlearning. (2008, June 24). *Fostering learning in the networked world: The cyberlearning opportunity and challenge*. Retrieved from http://www.nsf.gov/pubs/2008/nsf08204/nsf08204.pdf

Northern Arizona University. (2013). *Five-year strategic plan FY 2014–2018*. Retrieved from http://nau.edu/President/Strategic_Plan/

Palmer, C. (2012, October 1). Lecture theatres to go the way of the dodo. *The Conversation*. Retrieved from http://theconversation.com/lecture-theatres-to-go-the-way -of-the-dodo-9893

Rowley, D., & Sherman, H. (2001). *From strategy to change: Implementing the plan in higher education*. San Francisco, CA: Jossey-Bass.

Shank, P. (Ed.). (2007). *The online learning idea book: 95 proven ways to enhance technology-based and blended learning*. San Francisco, CA: Pfeiffer.

Sorcinelli, M., Austin, A., Eddy, P., & Beach, A. (2006). *Creating the future of faculty development: Learning from the past, understanding the present*. Bolton, MA: Anker Publishing Company.

U.S. Department of Education. (2009). *Evaluation of evidence-based practices in online learning: A meta-analysis and review of online learning studies*. Washington, DC: Author.

The White House, Office of the Press Secretary. (2013, August 22). *Remarks by the President on college affordability*. Retrieved from http://www.whitehouse .gov/the-press-office/2013/08/22/remarks-president-college-affordability-buffalo-ny

Zhao, Y., Lei, J., Yan, B., Lai, C., & Tan, S. (2005). What makes the difference? A practical analysis of research on the effectiveness of distance education. *Teachers College Record, 107*(8), 1836–1884.

KIM VANDERLINDEN is an assistant professor in the Educational Leadership Department at Northern Arizona University.

8

This chapter highlights a variety of ways researchers use learning theories with respect to different stakeholder groups. The chapter brings together common themes across these areas and proposes ways to use these ideas for future research on learning.

Constructing an Overarching Framework for Learning—Connecting the Dots

Marilyn J. Amey

Some theorists (e.g., Kezar, 2005; Senge, 1996; Yukl, 2009) suggest that organizational learning is, in reality, a form of collective learning, but these authors do not always articulate how learning occurring across stakeholders translates into organizational learning. For example, Senge (1996) claims that deep organizational change requires a deep change in the people who are a part of that organization, but leaves open how to accomplish the requisite level of learning at the individual level that yields the desired institutional outcome. Not only is organizational learning a cumulative effect of the collaborative, but it also has a generative effect that creates greater overall gains.

When talking about members of an organization, especially students, we might be inclined to focus on the ways in which learning is transformative, emphasizing deep and significant change as a result of substantive interactions and experiences inside and outside the classroom. Transformative learning occurs when individuals change their perspective as a result of reflection that questions underlying assumptions (Mezirow, 1997). Wawrzynski and Baldwin (Chapter 5 of this volume), and others, argue that transformative learning occurs when people reconsider established frames of reference or understanding that no longer align with their lived reality or do not seem as useful as they once were. When learners experience this misalignment, they need to redefine their standpoint on a problem or situation to make the perspective "more inclusive, discriminating, open, reflective" (Cranton, 2006, p. 36), and adaptable. Transformative learning theory explains that learning occurs when an individual encounters an alternative perspective and prior habits of mind or mental models are called into question (Cranton, 2006).

New Directions for Higher Education, no. 165, Spring 2014 © 2014 Wiley Periodicals, Inc.
Published online in Wiley Online Library (wileyonlinelibrary.com) • DOI: 10.1002/he.20086

Although we often consider transformative learning in terms of students, similar arguments could be made for faculty and staff as Eddy (Chapter 2) and Zakrajsek (Chapter 6) do earlier in this volume, and for organizations as VanDerLinden (Chapter 7) argues. While we may not always want or need transformation, per se, we know that continued evolution is necessary for personal growth and development as it is for broader organizational health.

Many organizational theorists will talk about learning organizations perhaps more than they reference transformational organizations; at the base, concepts may be quite similar and the focus is on continuous learning as the means by which entities continue to survive (Bridges & Bridges, 2000; O'Banion, 1997; Senge, 1996; Vaill, 1997). Vaill (1997) argued that organizations and their leaders/members should operate from a learning premise, by which he means continually being challenged by new ideas, new problems, new strategies, new interpretations, and new opportunities. He goes on to state that the learning premise for organizations means being willing to continually reinterpret that which is assumed to be known and well understood. It is, in some ways, always to be a *beginner* and *beginning*, rather than striving to be the expert.

Therein lies one of the contradictions in the academy and the way in which it has long operated, and why the notion of a learning premise may be counterintuitive to some. As a student, for example, the curricular systems and processes emphasize mastery of knowledge and competencies, and funnel student interests into majors where they become "experts" in fields of study. Administrators and staff strive to be promoted and advance in their careers, which is often based on having mastered the system in which they are employed; for faculty, tenure and promotion in rank are typically tied to national and international reputations as a subject and scholarly expert; and for organizations, expertise might be seen in the constant quest for increased rankings and status mobility, or institutional drift (Fairweather, 2005). These oversimplified examples illustrate how accepting the mantle of beginner and continuously beginning may run against the norm in higher education, and therefore, interfere with developing a culture framed by a learning premise. The elementary illustrations so quickly accepted as normative in the academy can also diminish Vaill's (1997) point that this kind of learning is hard, and it is intentional, and therefore, sought or purposely initiated, rather than something assumed to just occur naturally.

Yet, if we can embrace the idea of the learning premise and the learning organization, then it becomes clear that without organizational learning, we are far less likely to improve the operations and processes on college campuses that foster learning for students, faculty, and administrators. This chapter considers how to connect the dots of the postsecondary learning enterprise, identifying what is common in learning across levels of the institution, what differs, and how concepts of learning theory from specific focal points can expand how we think about learning in general. Arriving at an integrative framework highlights connections between learning theories applied at different organizational levels and how these connections lead, or at least should lead, to organizational learning.

Key Issues in Organizational Learning

The prospective integrative framework for organizational learning that follows builds on key learning issues identified elsewhere in this volume and casts them in terms of organizational functioning. A challenge in connecting the dots of learning across levels of an organization and its multiple constituents is one of language used to describe and label what is happening. While what follows continues to be grounded in organizational literature, it pulls also from language and ideas found in research on learning as it relates to students, faculty, and administrators.

Breaking Tradition/Paradox of Organizational Culture. One of the key features of organizational learning has to do with breaking tradition and challenging organizational culture. We need context in order to situate learning, and in the case of organizational learning, context is provided by culture—how we understand our institution, how it functions, what it values, and so forth. Even though culture provides foundation for our understanding and meaning construction, it can also get in the way; hence, the paradox of culture (Amey & Brown, 2004; Senge, 1996, Yukl, 2009). Culture is often subconscious or unconscious, and the mental models that guide our actions are not quickly challenged or even necessarily acknowledged.

We have to be willing to question the basic assumptions that guide our work and give it meaning in order to actually learn (Handy, 2002; Senge, 1996). If we are not able or willing to challenge these foundations, as those promoted by and through the system as exemplars of it typically are not inclined to do (Senge, 1996), it causes problems for organizational learning. Interrogating embedded assumptions and beliefs, however, can also result in disequilibrium and disorienting dilemmas (Chapman & Randall, 2007; Heifetz, 1994), regression, disenfranchisement, and stagnation. In order to promote and engage in learning, members need to deconstruct their understanding of organizational culture so that they see the possibilities of new knowledge and perspectives.

Moving Away From Quick Fixes and Easy Answers. Especially for institutional leaders under pressure to respond to external shifts in the environment and increasing public scrutiny, there is considerable demand to act. Not only is this action perpetuated by external forces, but it is frequently the criteria by which we judge our leaders and peers within the organization—did they *do* something? A key to organizational learning is moving away from easy answers and just fixing things, and developing potential throughout the organization to see various levels and forms of real-life problem solving as opportunities for *learning*.

This change in orientation rarely comes because the slogan of being learning focused shows up on business cards. Innovation, questioning how we have always done things, and pushing back on output-only assignments that do not cultivate better process models are not easy when it goes against the culture to do so (Argyris & Schön, 1978). This shift may be hardest to "sell" as an idea to senior leaders who can believe they already know what is best, who have created a culture where they are less able to appear vulnerable, and where they allow experience to substitute fully for critical thinking and reflection (Senge, 1996).

Adaptive work and learning: The idea of moving away from easy answers and quick fixes mirrors Heifetz's (1994) concept of adaptive work, where he distinguishes between problems for which answers are readily known and strategies easily identifiable and those which require new ways of thinking. Technical problems are not inconsequential, nor are they even easy. But the responses come from that which we already know and have within our repertoire—the "quick fix." When the problem is not well understood, as is true for many higher education institutions today, one needs adaptive strategies (Heifetz, 1994). In these situations where solutions are not already known, leaders including presidents, provosts, deans, directors, classroom faculty, and residence hall directors give the work back to those involved because learning will be needed in order to address the problem.

The significance of adaptive work for organizational learning cannot be overstated; rather than vesting answers, strategies, and problem solving in the most senior leaders and in limited response sets, adaptive work involves members throughout in challenging and changing their beliefs, values, attitudes, and behaviors (Chapman & Randall, 2007; Heifetz, 1994). Learning new ways of being is required, which is challenging and uncomfortable, and often not how the processes and reporting structures of the organization have been set up. Responses to the adaptive challenges can come from anywhere and the learning required to appropriately address these dilemmas is synergistic and generative.

In principle, Heifetz's (1994) adaptive work is similar to how Mezirow (1996) talks about learning—differentiating between instrumental learning (meaning to control the environment or other people) and communicative learning (seeking the meaning and significance of assumptions, beliefs, and values; as cited in Chapman & Randall, 2007, p. 53). Examining previously held assumptions, subconscious ideas and propositions, and making conscious one's mental maps (Senge, 1990) are the foundation of adult learning according to Mezirow (1996) and also of organizational learning (Argyris & Schön, 1978; Handy, 2002; Senge, 1990). The critical reflection required to accomplish this kind of learning allows for more inclusive frames of reference, incorporation of new ways of thinking and knowing, and the possibility of transformation. In this volume, Barber (Chapter 1) speaks about microsteps as the incremental progress in learning while Eddy (Chapter 2) speaks of transformational learning experiences. From an organizational perspective, both are likely necessary for ongoing development. Both require catalysts for critical reflection that leads to dissonance and disequilibrium; both require some means of support and degree of agency of individuals to be accomplished; both represent a blend or integration of continuity and innovation. Yet, the processes and initiatives for incremental and transformative learning may differ, and need to be better understood in order to be effectively facilitated.

It is important to focus on the meaning in order for the learning to occur, because the organizational structures are what get challenged and changed in the process of adaptive work or transformation. Chapman and Randall (2007) argue that there is a close relationship between Mezirow's (1996) and Heifetz's (1994) theories, although Mezirow focuses on the individual level and Heifetz on the collective; they both concur, however, that organizations learn only through individuals who learn even while individual learning does not guarantee organizational learning (Senge, 1990).

Feedback and Reflection.   An important part of organizational learning, as is true for individual learning, is feedback and reflection. Feedback does not just mean information, even though understanding how organizational members acquire knowledge is a valuable question. Nor should it be assumed that transparency means learning has occurred, so feedback requires more than just making information available. Mezirow (1997) claims that transformative learning takes place within the context of group dialogue. Structured and informal discussions and conversations that evaluate experiences, clarify beliefs and values, and articulate feelings can promote thoughtful examination, and reconsideration of frames of reference, and can help organizational members achieve deeper understandings of their organizations, what they are trying to accomplish, and why (Mezirow, 1997).

Dialogue requires listening to others and to self, as well, which can promote careful and thoughtful reflection through which members question long-standing beliefs and unexamined assumptions as a result of new experiences, taking into account alternate perspectives of others and seeing issues from multiple perspectives (Amey & Brown, 2004; Preskill & Brookfield, 2009; Wawrzynski & Baldwin, Chapter 5 of this volume). Vaill (1997) describes this as learning to analyze one's experiences and the interpretations of others. Engaging in this kind of questioning and multiperspective dialogue can challenge others to see complexities and interrelationships beyond one's sphere and comfort zone (Preskill & Brookfield, 2009). From a learning perspective, leaders need to find ways to engage members of their units and organizations.

Leaders in organizations may need to provide the space for thinking, reflecting, trying on new ideas, transitions, internalizing new understandings, and institutionalizing new processes just as classroom teachers know these steps are important in student learning. Yet, it is also important to recognize that the disequilibrium that can be caused by change initiatives to prompt deep learning take time, are hard work, and are often very discomforting (Bridges & Bridges, 2000; Senge, 1996; Vaill, 1997). This suggests a need for a holding environment (Heifetz, 1994) or neutral space (Amey & Brown, 2004) that offers a chance to metaphorically catch one's breath, reflect, and work through the dissonance. Reminiscent of Sanford's (1962) challenge and support, the ability to navigate the tension caused by this kind of deep learning for different stakeholders is central to successfully moving to incorporating new ideas and learning. But leading through this transition (Bridges & Bridges, 2000) means that leaders have to be prepared to modulate and mediate the conflicting perspectives—the organizational "noise"—and adjust the provocations for the needs of the diverse constituent learners (Kolb, 1998).

Learning Infrastructure.   Accomplishing these key strategies of organizational learning requires constructing a learning infrastructure or the support systems that foster people's willingness to take risks and learn (Senge, 1996; Van Velsor & Guthrie, 2003). This means relationships and processes that help people receive and hear the information they need to hear, understand the meaning of the information, figure out development plans, persist in their growth and learning, and then have the courage to question (and change) outmoded behaviors and attitudes (Van Velsor & Guthrie, 2003). Support can mean providing a network of those who have experience with similar situations, who are also new to a given task, or working with a veteran with experience (Van Velsor & Guthrie, 2003).

It may mean bridging silos and departments, but it may also require helping members find the support networks they need in order to truly learn. Barber (Chapter 1 of this volume) says in order to create a larger theory of learning that might have multiple applications, it will be necessary to eliminate some of the institutional and organizational barriers to integration of learning (e.g., silos, organizational structures like budget accounting systems, rank, authorship). While using different language, he could be referring to learning infrastructures that promote risk taking and learning. So the question becomes what learning is required of organizations to do the things espoused throughout this volume? Are there organizational equivalents of Leslie's (Chapter 4 of this volume) orthogonal outcomes that cut across organizational silos and make boundaries more permeable? If so, how would we organize differently, and what would we be doing, to achieve the learning outcomes articulated for students, faculty, and administrators?

The Importance of Intentionality

Actions and initiatives may have unintended effects, but there needs to be a sense of intentionality if one expects the organization to have the ability to evolve and learn collectively (e.g., participating, socializing, bringing back information to those who do not participate). As mentioned, initiating meaningful dialogues, developing support structures, and providing feedback and the time and space for reflection in order to make meaning of the circumstances require time and conscious effort, and must be built into organizations if learning is to occur. When experiences are intentional, learning can become comprehensive, holistic, and potentially transformative. VanDerLinden (Chapter 7 of this volume) points to the role of intentionality in designing institutional strategy to promote blended learning and argues how organizational learning emerges which leads to transformation.

When thinking about the college experience in and out of the classroom, we recognize the importance of not causing students to forage for meaning and understanding on their own, and instead we identify ways of providing intentional learning experiences that support and challenge appropriately in a community. With faculty, we focus on early career faculty support after which we do less once faculty members are post-tenure, assuming there is nothing left for faculty members to learn. When administrators join the organization or start a new job, we hand out job descriptions, office manuals, and keys, and assume somehow everyone figures it out and "learns" on their own. How different might it be if organizations intentionally developed high-impact learning experiences for faculty and administrators which are advocated for classroom learning? If we took a holistic approach to capacity building for all employees? If we assessed supervisors and leaders based on how they intentionally construct learning and capacity building experiences for others and not just on output?

As we contemplate how to move toward more holistic learning across the institution, perhaps we can invoke organizational aspirations offered by De Pree (1997): "A place of realized potential opens itself to change, to contrary opinion, to the mystery of potential, to involvement, to unsettling ideas. They offer people a place to learn and to grow" (p. 11).

References

Amey, M. J., & Brown, D. F. (2004). *Breaking out of the box: Interdisciplinary collaboration and faculty work*. Charlotte, NC: Greenwood Press/Information Age Publishing.

Argyris, C., & Schön, D. A. (1978). *Organizational learning: A theory of action perspective*. Reading, MA: Addison-Wesley.

Bridges, W., & Bridges, S. M. (2000). Leading transition: A new model for change. *Leader to Leader Journal, 16*, 30–36. Retrieved from http://www.hesselbeininstitute.org/knowledgecenter/journal.aspx?ArticleID=28

Chapman, S. A., & Randall, L. M. (2007). Adaptive leadership and transformative learning: A case study of leading by part-time faculty. In J. F. Wergin (Ed.), *Leadership in place: How academic professionals can find their leadership voice* (pp. 51–75). San Francisco, CA: Anker Publishing Company.

Cranton, P. (2006). *Professional development as transformative learning: New perspectives for teachers of adults*. San Francisco, CA: Jossey-Bass.

De Pree, M. (1997). Places of realized potential. In M. De Pree (Ed.), *Leading without power: Finding hope in serving community* (pp. 9–20). San Francisco, CA: Jossey-Bass.

Fairweather, J. S. (2005). Beyond rhetoric: Trends in the relative value of teaching and learning in faculty salaries. *The Journal of Higher Education, 76*(4), 401–422.

Handy, C. (2002). Elephants and fleas: Is your organization prepared for change? *Leader to Leader Journal, 24,* 29–34.

Heifetz, R. A. (1994). *Leadership without easy answers.* Cambridge, MA: Harvard University Press.

Kezar, A. J. (Ed.). (2005). *New Directions for Higher Education: No. 139. Organizational learning in higher education.* San Francisco, CA: Jossey-Bass.

Kolb, D. A. (1998). Learning styles and disciplinary differences. In K. A. Feldman & M. B. Paulsen (Eds.), *Teaching and learning in the college classroom* (pp. 127–137). Needham Heights, MA: Simon & Schuster.

Mezirow, J. (1996). Contemporary paradigms of learning. *Adult Education Quarterly, 46*(3), 158–172.

Mezirow, J. (1997). Transformative learning: Theory to practice. In P. Cranton (Ed.), *New Directions for Adult and Continuing Education: No. 74. Higher education: A global community* (pp. 5–12). San Francisco, CA: Jossey-Bass.

O'Banion, T. A. (1997). *A learning college for the 21st Century.* Washington, DC: American Council on Education.

Preskill, S., & Brookfield, S. D. (2009). *Learning as a way of leading: Lessons from the struggle for social justice.* San Francisco, CA: Jossey-Bass.

Sanford, N. (1962). *The American college.* New York, NY: Wiley.

Senge, P. M. (1990). *The fifth discipline: The art and practice of the learning organization.* New York, NY: Currency Doubleday.

Senge, P. M. (1996). The ecology of leadership. *Leader to Leader Journal, 2,* 18–23. Retrieved from http://www.hesselbeininstitute.org/knowledgecenter/journal.aspx?ArticleID=137

Vaill, P. B. (1997). The learning challenges of leadership. In B. Adams & S. Webster (Eds.), *The balance of leadership and followership working papers* (Kellogg Leadership Studies Project; pp. 71–86). College Park, MD: Academy of Leadership Press, University of Maryland.

Van Velsor, E., & Guthrie, V. A. (2003). Enhancing the ability to learn from experience. In J. Gallos (Ed.), *Business leadership: A Jossey-Bass reader* (pp. 223–247). San Francisco, CA: Jossey-Bass.

Yukl, G. (2009). Leading organizational learning: Reflections on theory and research. *The Leadership Quarterly, 20*(1), 49–53.

MARILYN J. AMEY *is a professor of higher, adult, and lifelong education and chairperson of the Department of Educational Administration at Michigan State University.*

9

Learning is a core part of all forms of higher education work. College leaders of all kinds—administrators, staff, faculty, and students—must know how to seek out and support the wide array of learning that can go on in colleges and universities.

Finding and Fostering Learning: What College and University Leaders Need to Know and What They Can Do

Anna Neumann, Liza Bolitzer

Briefly scanning the table of contents of this volume highlights a significant feature of higher education that we often take for granted: Learning surrounds us. It is a central element of virtually all work that goes on in colleges and universities. Students and faculty are tasked with learning in their disciplines and fields. Faculty are charged with learning how to teach, advise, and mentor. College and university leaders must regularly update their knowledge of challenges and opportunities—locally, nationally, and worldwide—as these will shape what higher education is and can be. All entrants to higher education must learn the local and larger professional work processes, ethos, cultures, and politics that define their specialized fields, specific workplaces, and academe at large.

But there is more to consider. Time brings large-scale change—demographic, cultural, political, technological—that shapes what higher education can offer to society at any one point. This kind of broad change forces questions such as: Who are our students today, and what does each student, uniquely, bring here that she or he can deploy toward their learning academically, socially, and personally? What social, cultural, political, scientific, and human wonders and accomplishments, dangers and disasters, and opportunities and challenges frame the kind of learning in which our students would do well to engage, and that our college can promote? Given the range of political and economic changes currently apace in the nation and the world, and locally in the state or region, what do college administrators need to know to support the substantive learning that their college strives for? What must college presidents, trustees, donors, legislators, federal officials, and philanthropists understand—about students,

New Directions for Higher Education, no. 165, Spring 2014 © 2014 Wiley Periodicals, Inc.
Published online in Wiley Online Library (wileyonlinelibrary.com) • DOI: 10.1002/he.20087

faculty, society, culture, economics, and history—to help all college members do their work well and thereby enact their institution's charter to advance learning?

These questions underscore a simple fact about higher education: All people associated with higher education learn—students, instructors, student personnel specialists, college secretarial and clerical staff, facilities workers, administrators, and trustees—as do many external actors, including the families of today's college students, voters, state and federal policymakers, state legislators, elected officials, and members of the general public. Although *what* these people learn about higher education differs, all learn one thing or another (e.g., see Neumann, 2009). All work with what they know already, and to some extent, all raise questions about what they are learning and the process of learning itself.

Given the pervasiveness of learning within colleges and universities and leaders' needs to support and steer core institutional processes, including learning, we discuss three issues in this chapter: (a) the complexity of learning; (b) what learning is and what leaders need to know about it in order to see, find, and understand it; and (c) how leaders may foster learning college-wide.

Learning From the Perspective of College Leadership

As detailed elsewhere in this volume, learning occurs in many corners of higher education: in classrooms, residence halls, dining areas, student activity rooms, faculty members' and administrators' offices, labs, faculty conference rooms, and trustees' meeting rooms. These days, learning of this sort extends beyond the campus as well—into the living rooms of people contemplating college enrollment for themselves or their family members.

But the proposition that learning surrounds us, infiltrating just about everything that goes on in higher education, is also daunting. First, if people throughout a college are indeed learning, then it is likely that what they learn, why they learn, and how well or deeply they learn will vary. Second, persons and groups in the college are likely to learn in different ways, and they will require different supports for their learning. Some of these supports may be, literally, around the corner, but the learners may not know this. Some may be out of reach. Third, each learner, and each learning experience, projects its own sense of urgency. Some learners call for support immediately and consistently. Others, equally in need, struggle quietly. How is a leader to respond to so much learning—and to orchestrate it?

One response to these questions is that researchers in higher education and the social sciences have to date contributed many helpful concepts and perspectives for helping leaders, teachers, staff, and others understand leadership; many of the preceding chapters offer examples of such work. Yet this does not resolve the larger question: What's a leader to do with this panoply of learning, and also with the expansive array of theories for thinking about its diverse forms?

NEW DIRECTIONS FOR HIGHER EDUCATION • DOI: 10.1002/he

To help address this question in an era when learning is of high necessity—given the extent of change around us—we offer below several guidelines for orchestrating learning in a college or university. But first, we must pause to discuss what leadership means with regard to learning. We see leaders as using their skills, insights, and opportunities to understand, support, coordinate, and advance the learning of others with whom they work toward a common goal (Bensimon & Neumann, 1993). In this view, college presidents, vice presidents, deans, department chairs, and others in formal administrative positions are leaders—but so, too, are teachers, students, and college staff who seek to advance the knowing and learning of others with whom they work toward common goals that, first and foremost, demand understanding (Neumann & Larson, 1997). How may these leaders support others' learning, or position it for best effect? How may leaders keep these many forms of learning—as well as the different learning agendas of different actors—from colliding with one another or from overrunning each other's? How can leaders identify, understand, and appreciate good and generative learning—and how can they use it, given that it may occur, unseen and unheard, in multiple college or university corners?

We suggest that to lead an organization where diverse learning—by diverse people and about diverse subjects—goes on, leaders must, first and foremost, be able to recognize it—to know it when they see it. They also must respect people's efforts to learn regardless of whether their learning turns out well or badly (learning involves making mistakes and hopefully learning from them; see Neumann, 1990). They must appreciate that learners, being human, will be limited in how much they can know and learn (Birnbaum, 1988; Cohen & March, 1974; March & Simon, 1958; Simon, 1997), and in what they can see or sense, given the opportunities and constraints that they and others create at any point in time (Greeno, Collins, & Resnick, 1996; Weick, 1979). Given what they do discern, about others' learning, leaders must then act thoughtfully and respectfully to support and advance the learning of all.

Finding Learning: What It Is, and What Leaders Need to Know About It

In this section, we offer a brief protocol that leaders can use to help them *begin to take notice* of the many forms of learning that go on around them. We use the words *taking notice* because learning—by the many different people who engage in it, and also by the leaders who seek to understand these persons' efforts—requires sustained and systematic effort on everyone's part. When learning goes on, the "stuff" that people try to learn usually shifts from moment to moment. Learning suggests that what learners think about does not stand still (Bransford, Brown, & Cocking, 2000). Due to this flux, it is hard to grasp *what it is* that learners know at any moment, and it is hard to spot—much less track—their coming to know over time. Further we use the word *begin* because visualizing others' learning, in ways that really "get at it," is a process. Learning is evanescent. To spot it, credibly, leaders must dedicate time, thought, and persistence to so doing.

To take notice of learning requires that leaders "know it when they see it"—or for that matter, when they hear it. Sometimes leaders recognize learning instantaneously. At other times, they struggle, wondering if what they're looking at is learning, or an illusion of it. This raises the obvious question: If learning can truly be hard to spot, much less follow, how can leaders identify it credibly? What are some signs of learning? What should leaders take notice of in examining learning? Where should they look, and what for? We address these basic but important questions with guidance from theories of how people learn in schools (Bransford et al., 2000; Shulman, 2004a, 2004b) and in higher education settings (Birnbaum, 1988; Neumann, 2012), and by drawing on studies of organizational cognition broadly (Cohen & March, 1974; Hodgkinson & Healey, 2008; Weick, 1979).

To learn is to surface, reflect on, question, and often reformulate what one knows already, or what one assumes about an idea, perspective, fact, event, or point of interest (Bransford et al., 2000; Dewey, 1902, 1916; Shulman, 2004a, 2004b). A person who openly surfaces and questions what she or he knows or believes already is engaging in a very challenging task. To question one's own knowing—what one takes as real or worthwhile—requires courage, tolerance for confusion, and often humility on the part of the learner (Birnbaum, 1988; Neumann, 2014).

But there is more to say, since in learning the onus is not and cannot be only on the learner. To learn, a person must have an opportunity to do so, ideally with a teacher (or teacher figure) who deeply understands the learner and the stuff being learned, and who creates bridges between the two (Neumann, 1995a, 1995b; Shulman, 2004a, 2004b). Large-scale conditions also shape people's learning—sometimes instantaneously as in wartime, or amid environmental disasters—but at other times, slowly, historically, for example, as emerging technologies reshape what it means to go to school. In this view, contexts are "teachers" too. Just as contexts contribute to the content and quality of children's "prior learning" as starting points for their formal learning in schools (Gonzalez, Moll, & Amanti, 2005), so do contexts shape what faculty, staff, and others believe, sometimes deeply, about their colleges (Neumann, 1995a, 1995b). Just as teachers must work with the prior knowledge that children bring to school to help them achieve understanding, so must new leaders work with the prior knowledge of the people whose understandings they hope to shape through their leadership.

We must then wonder how college leaders might spot such learning as it occurs amid the complex, fast-paced social, political, and cultural contexts that comprise today's campuses. Given that colleges employ, sponsor, and serve many different kinds of people occupying diverse roles—each charged with doing and learning many different things—one can ask: What might a leader look for, in terms of learning, in searching for it? What should a leader know about learning to be able to spot any of its features? We address this question by drawing on insights from current research in the cognitive sciences and sociocultural studies to present some key features of learning. Alongside each feature, we present guiding questions that leaders can use to search for learning in light of that feature.

Learning Means Learning Some *Thing*.   Learning assumes the existence of *a thing* to be known, or to be known more deeply, accurately, or completely than it has been in the past (Dewey, 1902, 1916; Palmer, 2007). Learning will not occur independent of the thing being learned. For college students, the thing being learned may be a disciplinary idea, or a concept central to being an adult in a democratic society—for example, civic responsibility, moral courage, compassion, or altruism. For faculty, the thing to be learned may be a discipline's "breaking news," or approaches to teaching a field's new ideas. For administrators and trustees, that thing to be learned might be ways of thinking through the politics of a budgeting process, a faculty's culture and values, or the state's concerns around accountability.

Questions for leaders to consider: If learning is going on, then people are learning some thing or things in particular. Learning assumes an object being learned or grappled with. To locate learning in a particular space, it sometimes helps to find that object first. Thus a leader can ask: What in particular is being learned in this instance?

Learning as *Someone* Engaged in Learning.   Learning does not happen without one or more people or groups engaging in it. Who those people are shapes the learning that occurs (Neumann, 2005; Schwab, 1983; Wenger, 1999). For example, when students learn, they bring their prior knowledge, gained in and out of schools in the past, into the new learning situation. Ideally, they surface some of that past knowledge, comparing it to a new idea, hopefully addressing discrepancies between old and new (Bransford et al., 2000; Shulman, 2004a, 2004b). Learning is, therefore, about what goes on in people's consciousness as they move between what they once knew and what they can potentially now know. It is person-centered to its core.

Questions for leaders to consider: A leader may seek to identify who it is who is learning, or trying to learn in a given situation. The leader may then consider: Who is involved in learning in this space? That leader also might ask: What might be the relationship of learners to one another in this setting? What does each one bring to the learning experience?

Learning as Occurring in *Contexts*.   Learning occurs within contexts (environments, milieux, and settings) that shape whatever it is that learners seek to know. The particular setting in which learning materializes frames how the learning proceeds in the experiences of the people it touches—for example, as it affords unique forms of access to learning, or as it sets up constraints on it. Thus, contexts frame individuals' and groups' opportunities to learn (Gutierrez & Rogoff, 2003; Lee, 2007; Schwab, 1983; Wortham, 2006). For example, to consider the contexts likely to shape the learning of faculty members in a particular disciplinary department, a leader could consider: the state of the discipline's development or its availability as a resource for learning on this particular campus; the full range of social, historical, cultural, economic, and political forces influencing this discipline at this time; the formal and informal networks, groups, and communities within which individual faculty members participate; the particular people and situations in faculty members' lives, including colleagues, students, friends, partners, and others, all of whom influence what learners put their minds to (see Alemán, 2010; Bronfenbrenner, 1979; Gutierrez & Rogoff, 2003; Neumann & Peterson, 1997). While leaders cannot and should not get into all these spaces, they are advised to understand that what any person learns is likely to be shaped by them all.

Questions for leaders to consider: What is the nature of the locale within which the learning we've identified is occurring? What boundaries mark off the space in which this learning occurs? How can I characterize that space with regard to the learning that goes on there?

Learning Brings People, Things, and Contexts *Together*. Having identified particular individuals who appear to be learning particular ideas, issues, or skills, and having clarified the specific locations within which their learning appears to take place, leaders will want to confirm these initial suppositions. To do so, leaders can return to the preceding questions, pursuing them again but more deeply. They may ask: What evidence exists in this locale, among the people here, that suggests they are learning? To address this question, leaders can reuse the three guiding questions, this time digging deeply to question the authenticity of learning identified earlier.

Thus for the basic question—*If people in this particular site are learning, what exactly are they learning?*—leaders in search of learning can follow with: How can we know, with more certainty, what exactly it is that people here are learning? What evidence of their learning this thing in particular exists? And more deeply: What is the range of the learning that goes on here about this thing, and where does it stop? How far do learners in this site go in their learning of it? How deeply are they pushing into it? How imaginative is their thinking about it? What's "new" in what they learn about it? How do learners test the quality of their learning of it?

Leaders may then follow with a second look at the second question— *So who among the people in this site appear to be engaged in learning?* How do we know that we have accounted for all learners, and in fact, that all those named are learning? How does the learning of particular things (per above) vary from person to person, or from group to group, and why? How linked is it? If people in this site vary in their learning, what is the nature of their variance—especially relative to who people are and what they do?

And not least, to probe context, leaders may ask: *What is the nature of the site in which this particular learning is happening?* Which work structures and processes does it include? Which members of this site are aware of the learning that goes on here, and which are not? Which members participate in it, and which do not? What is the nature of the culture—its ethos, rituals, routines, rhythms, and patterns—of this space? What local ideas seem to frame the learning that goes on here?

Learning—about others' learning—takes time. Further, leaders must themselves do the learning at issue; they cannot delegate learning—for example, about organizational members' learning—to others.

With insights into college-wide learning in hand, gained through investigations like the ones we describe above, leaders are positioned to take their next steps toward fostering and strengthening learning college-wide. We offer some guidelines for this in the next section.

Fostering Learning: A Protocol for Cultivating Learning College-Wide

In this section, we continue to lay out the findings of learning research, first as strategic actions that leaders can take toward fostering learning campuswide, and then as questions that may help them frame their actions.

Fostering Access to Learning.   Learning occurs both within and between individuals (Wenger, 1999). It occurs in individual experience but extends outwardly into others'. Though reaching outwardly, learning is bounded—both by the natural limitations of learners' minds, and by the cultural, political, and physical dynamics that shape (and thereby constrain) human relationship (March & Simon, 1958; Simon, 1997; Weick, 1979). Thus, learning creates insiders and outsiders to it. Much like teachers, leaders would do well to extend learning, in its many forms, to all the persons whose thinking they strive to lead. Doing that can be challenging.

In seeking to foster access to learning, leaders can draw from experiences of teachers who negotiate access within their classrooms. Consider, as a case in point, two first-year students in an introductory philosophy class. One student is a movie buff. The first student comments frequently, often drawing on favorite films to think through big philosophical ideas. When this student shares thoughts in class, other peers, many of whom have seen the same films, chime in. The other student has just completed military service. The second student uses this experience as a soldier—traveling, engaging in conflict, encountering diverse cultures—as reference points for the thoughts shared in class about issues of morality and power that the philosophy texts raise. The second student's comments, unfamiliar to the other younger students, often elicit an awkward silence in class. Looking around this classroom, we note several students who say little, or whose comments, like the veteran's, are rarely picked up by classmates. Viewed together, the unique comments of the movie buff and veteran, and several others' silence suggest that each person in this classroom brings distinct knowledge, and distinct ways of understanding the world, to his or her reading and thinking of new academic material. It is sometimes hard for students to articulate their thoughts, wedged as they are between textualized ideas and personal experience.

Enter the instructor who appreciates the role that prior knowledge plays in encounters with new and powerful ideas like those that students discuss. This teacher carefully notes which of the students' ideas (and prior experiences) are pulled into discussion, and which are left out. The teacher monitors too who speaks and who does not and reaches out to interact with students to whom others rarely respond. At times, the teacher links something that a hesitant speaker offers to a point that a more frequent speaker makes, bringing them both onto the same plane. This action allows students to speak in pairs and groups. The teacher continues to talk with students after class ends, at times, waiting patiently for students' words.

Although this example focuses on students' efforts to learn subject-matter ideas in class, much the same goes on within faculty, staff, and administrator discussions—though about different topics. The strategies we illustrate here—for example, a teacher opening up to widely varying student experiences and understandings, then teaching students to do the same with their peers—apply as well to leaders as they work with faculty and staff.

Questions for leaders to consider: Who is included in the learning that goes on here? Who is not? What rationales underlie inclusion and exclusion? What kinds of things seem to be getting in the way of meaningful and inclusive participation in this learning? How might I foster inclusiveness?

Fostering Choice in Learning.   Sometimes the best a leader can do is open doors for choice in learning. At times what blocks people's learning is not a specific interpersonal dynamic, but rather a social structural pattern that grows slowly and wordlessly over longer stretches of time. Embedded in daily life, it may be hard to see and name.

Consider this example: Amid research on recently tenured professors' learning in the sciences, Anna Neumann interviewed a number of female scientists who, in addition to engaging in research, were spending significant time working through the human dynamics of scientific work groups, faculty and administrator politics, and classroom and curricular problems (Neumann, 2009; Terosky, Phifer, & Neumann, 2008). It was hard to tell whether the women chose purposefully to concentrate on the human and political side of the enterprise to the point that doing so reshaped how they thought about science, or whether others positioned them, wordlessly and perhaps unconsciously, to do that work.

In one case, a woman scientist found herself engaged extensively in "political" organizational work while her male colleagues devoted themselves to substantive scientific endeavors slated to turn into publications. The woman had not actively chosen the larger contextual-political endeavor (taking care of the people side of the enterprise), and found her positioning, years into this effort, both interesting and irksome. This is not to say that orchestrating the people side of a scientific or academic endeavor is not interesting or important. But in some cases, like this one, doing so—without consciously choosing to, especially when others in equivalent positions do exercise conscious choice—cuts short individuals' opportunities to learn. It also cuts short the opportunities of these individuals' communities to learn from them. Given more choice, the woman might have contributed differently to her science, and her male colleagues might have learned too—about how to share in the work and learning of professional settings. This example raises questions about who has choice and control in learning, as well as what a leader can do to foster both for all learners (students, faculty, administrators, and staff) on campus.

Questions for leaders to consider: Who in this setting has choice—or over the years, has had choice—in their learning, and who does not, or has not? What customs or rules, explicit or implicit, might explain distinct patterns of participation? To what extent might established patterns of participation be impeding learning, and what might I do to address these?

Fostering Connection.   Leaders are usually better positioned to see and to explore individual and group-level learning than are other organizational members. This means that leaders may be able to spot overlaps or resonances in learning across individuals or groups who work in different parts of an institution, or outside it. It has been said that faculty and staff often work in "silos," largely unaware of what others around them are doing. It is possible that the escalated pace of life and work today coupled with the growing demands of "hard times"—both of which call for deep, intensive attention to one's own work—makes silos inevitable. Leaders who make strategic use of communication tools and systems—so that they have access to what's being worked on at "ground level"—have the capacity to see possibilities for synergies, colearning, and other forms of collaboration.

Questions for leaders to consider: Looking across the various sites of learning we've detected on this campus, where do we see overlaps, or potential for colearning, or possibilities for synergy? Which groups are grappling with similar or related questions, or struggling to understand the same thing, but from different angles? Where and how might individuals or groups, from different parts of this organization, come together? What can we do to facilitate that?

Fostering Public Understanding of Learning.   Enhanced public understanding of learning should focus on what it takes to learn and to advance learning by way of teaching. Higher education is in the public eye in ways it never has been before (see, e.g., the college scorecard at http://collegecost.ed.gov/scorecard/index.aspx). The higher education system, including the communities that comprise it and the individuals who enact it, are being called to account—most notably these days, for quantity and quality of student learning (Arum & Roksa, 2011). In this new environment, it is critical that leaders both "tighten up the ship" internally, improving the quality of teaching that goes on inside colleges and universities, and set up processes to support continuous educational improvement.

But there is more that leaders can do: They can dedicate themselves to educating the public, including policymakers and public officials, as to what learning is, what it demands of teachers and students, and how, where, and when it may materialize—indeed, in different ways, in different subjects of study, in different learners' experiences, in different institutions, and in different times (Neumann, 2014). Leaders may have to go further—for example, when assessment processes are so out of line with what it takes to teach well that they threaten to undo the very activity being assessed—namely teaching as an activity that seeks, intentionally, to promote learning. In doing so, assessment can threaten learning rather than improve it. Part of what may be at issue is weak understanding of teaching and assessment—on the part of the public, the media, and government leaders. Helping these audiences understand what it means to teach deeply and well for students' conceptual understanding, and helping them understand too what it means (and what it takes) to conduct assessment, are themselves grand acts of teaching. Leaders may have to learn to lead—by teaching—in this way.

Questions for leaders to consider: What questions, concerns, and expectations are policymakers and public leaders voicing about college students' learning? How well are public views of learning aligned with what learning looks and sounds like in college classrooms? What can I, as a college or university leader, contribute—and how might I help lead—the public conversation about what counts as good learning and teaching?

Closing Thoughts

These insights into learning, and into teaching that strives to foster it, are far from exhaustive. They should be viewed as starting points for building up learning as a feature of campus life. College and university leaders are advised to use them as guides for finding and fostering learning, as it materializes uniquely on their own campuses.

References

Alemán, A. (2010). College women's female friendships: A longitudinal view. *Journal of Higher Education, 81*(5), 553–582.

Arum, R., & Roksa, J. (2011). *Academically adrift: Limited learning on college campuses.* Chicago, IL: University of Chicago Press.

Bensimon, E. M., & Neumann, A. (1993). *Redesigning collegiate leadership: Teams and teamwork in higher education.* Baltimore, MD: The Johns Hopkins University Press.

Birnbaum, R. (1988). *How colleges work: The cybernetics of academic organization and leadership.* San Francisco, CA: Jossey-Bass.

Bransford, J. D., Brown, A. L., & Cocking, R. R. (Eds.). (2000). *How people learn: Brain, mind, experience, and school.* Washington, DC: National Academy Press.

Bronfenbrenner, U. (1979). *The ecology of human development: Experiments by nature and design.* Cambridge, MA: Harvard University Press.

Cohen, M. D., & March, J. G. (1974). *Leadership and ambiguity: The American college presidency*. New York, NY: McGraw-Hill.

Dewey, J. (1902). The child and the curriculum. In R. D. Archambault (Ed.), *John Dewey on education: Selected writings* (pp. 339–358). Chicago, IL: University of Chicago Press.

Dewey, J. (1916). The nature of subject matter. In R. D. Archambault (Ed.), *On education* (pp. 339–358). Chicago, IL: University of Chicago Press.

Gonzalez, N., Moll, L., & Amanti, C. (2005). *Funds of knowledge: Theorizing practices in households, communities, and classrooms*. Mahwah, NJ: Lawrence Erlbaum Associates.

Greeno, J., Collins, A., & Resnick, L. (1996). Cognition and learning. In D. Berliner & R. Calfee (Eds.), *Handbook of educational psychology* (pp. 15–46). New York, NY: Macmillan.

Gutierrez, K. D., & Rogoff, B. (2003). Cultural ways of learning: Individual traits or repertoires of practice. *Educational Researcher, 32*(5), 19–25.

Hodgkinson, G., & Healey, M. (2008). Cognition in organizations. *Annual Review of Psychology, 59,* 387–417.

Lee, C. (2007). *Culture, literacy, and learning: Taking bloom in the midst of the whirlwind*. New York, NY: Teachers College Press.

March, J. G., & Simon, H. (1958). *Organizations*. New York, NY: Wiley.

Neumann, A. (1990). Making mistakes: Error and learning in the college presidency. *The Journal of Higher Education, 61*(4), 386–407.

Neumann, A. (1995a). Context, cognition and culture: A case analysis of collegiate leadership and cultural change. *American Educational Research Journal, 32*(2), 251–279.

Neumann, A. (1995b). On the making of hard times and good times: The social construction of resource stress. *The Journal of Higher Education, 66*(1), 3–31.

Neumann, A. (2005). Observations: Taking seriously the topic of *learning* in studies of faculty work and careers. In E. G. Creamer & L. Lattuca (Eds.), *New Directions for Teaching and Learning: No. 102. Advancing faculty learning through interdisciplinary collaboration* (pp. 63–83). San Francisco, CA: Jossey-Bass.

Neumann, A. (2009). *Professing to learn: Creating tenured lives and careers in the American research university*. Baltimore, MD: The Johns Hopkins University Press.

Neumann, A. (2012). Organizational cognition in higher education. In M. Bastedo (Ed.), *The organization of higher education: Managing colleges for a new era* (pp. 304–331). Baltimore, MD: Johns Hopkins University Press.

Neumann, A. (2014). Staking a claim on learning: What we should know about learning in higher education, and why. *The Review of Higher Education, 37*(2), 249–267.

Neumann, A., & Larson, S. (1997). Enhancing the leadership factor in planning. In M. W. Peterson, D. D. Dill, & L. A. Mets (Eds.), *Planning and management for a changing environment: A handbook on redesigning postsecondary institutions* (pp. 191–203). San Francisco, CA: Jossey-Bass.

Neumann, A., & Peterson, P. L. (1997). *Learning from our lives: Women, research, and autobiography in education*. New York, NY: Teachers College Press.

Palmer, P. (2007). *The courage to teach*. San Francisco, CA: Jossey-Bass.

Schwab, J. J. (1983). The practical 4: Something for curriculum professors to do. *Curriculum Inquiry, 13*(3), 239–265.

Shulman, L. (2004a). *Teaching as community property: Essays on higher education*. San Francisco, CA: Jossey-Bass.

Shulman, L. (2004b). *The wisdom of practice: Essays on learning, teaching, and learning to teach*. San Francisco, CA: Jossey-Bass.

Simon, H. (1997). *Administrative behavior*. New York, NY: Free Press.

Terosky, A., Phifer, T., & Neumann, A. (2008). Shattering plexiglas: Continuing challenges for women professors in research universities. In J. Glazer-Raymo (Ed.), *Women in academe: The unfinished agenda* (pp. 52–79). Baltimore, MD: The Johns Hopkins Press.

Weick, K. (1979). *The social psychology of organizing* (2nd ed.). New York, NY: McGraw-Hill.

Wenger, E. (1999). *Communities of practice: Learning, meaning and identity*. New York, NY: Cambridge University Press.

Wortham, S. (2006). *Learning identity: The joint emergence of social identity and academic learning*. New York, NY: Cambridge University Press.

ANNA NEUMANN *is professor of higher education and chair of the Department of Organization and Leadership at Teachers College, Columbia University.*

LIZA BOLITZER *is a doctoral candidate and instructor of higher and postsecondary education at Teachers College, Columbia University.*

10

Interpersonal and transdisciplinary collaboration can facilitate and amplify the benefits of learning. Drawing from ideas presented throughout this volume, this culminating chapter describes ways to enhance collaborative learning within and among various stakeholder groups.

Bringing It All Together Through Group Learning

Shannon M. Chance

This volume has identified numerous ways to help postsecondary stakeholders learn more effectively. Drawing from existing literature related to "learning," each author has examined ways to push human knowledge forward by implementing innovative theories and pedagogical practices. This final chapter provides both a summary and a launch point for thinking about learning more broadly.

In doing so, this chapter: (a) identifies issues common to a variety of stakeholder groups, (b) discusses benefits of collaborative "group learning," (c) provides examples, and (d) presents two new models for fostering learning by promoting collaboration. The new models, generated through a phenomenological study of faculty collaboration that occurred at the Dublin Institute of Technology (DIT) in Ireland, may be useful in other educational environments where greater knowledge sharing is desired, be it among individuals, across programs, or at the institutional/organizational level (Chance, Duffy, Bowe, Murphy, & Duggan, 2013). The models are tools for organizational learning of the sort recommended by Moore and Mendez (Chapter 3 of this volume) because they adopt a systems perspective, conceptualize stakeholders as a "community of learners" (Kezar, 2005, p. 10), and suggest processes "for acquiring information, interpreting data, developing knowledge, and sustaining learning" (Kezar, 2005, p. 13) across the institution.

The models were built on the work of a small group of electrical engineering lecturers who sought to facilitate and support students' collaborative learning. They succeeded in fostering change in their classrooms, but they also influenced change program-wide. Today, they stand as precedent for others throughout their college, and are encouraged and supported in

NEW DIRECTIONS FOR HIGHER EDUCATION, no. 165, Spring 2014 © 2014 Wiley Periodicals, Inc.
Published online in Wiley Online Library (wileyonlinelibrary.com) • DOI: 10.1002/he.20088

leading change by college administrators. One major goal of this chapter is to show how the DIT model can help facilitate wide-scale integration of learning and foster transformative change.

The chapter helps address gaps in performance at the institutional/organizational level. Typical deficits in learning at this level include failure to learn from experience (Kolb, 1984, 1998; Presley & Leslie, 1999; Rowley, Lujan, & Dolence, 1997); failure to pool knowledge across disciplines, departments, and administrative units (Barber, Chapter 1 of this volume; Lauer, 2006); and failure to monitor plans and tweak performance (Holcomb, 2001; Wilson, 1997). As evidenced in the chapters of this volume, a lack of support for making connections and integrating topics hinders learning at all levels.

This chapter showcases how campus members can work together in a self-directed manner to foster continual learning and continually improved performance. By sharing ideas about learning that work within discrete stakeholder groups and applying them more broadly (i.e., across/among groups), we can connect learning across our institutions.

Core Questions and Best Practices

At the core of this volume lie questions like: How can leaders use methods that are known to facilitate transformational learning at the level of the individual and apply them to help groups learn more effectively—be these faculty groups or the organization at large? How can institutional leaders amplify positive effects that accrue from using innovative approaches to learning by "scaling them up" and applying them in more ways? To begin addressing such questions, let's review major points about learning discussed elsewhere in this volume, looking at each major stakeholder group individually and then assessing commonalities.

Whereas postsecondary institutions have traditionally focused on learning at the level of the student (in classrooms) and knowledge generation at the level of the faculty (through research and publication), there is a pressing need to do more to create and apply knowledge in service to society (Kerr, 1995), to learn from experience (Holcomb, 2001; Kolb, 1984, 1998), and to harness new techniques in order to perform more effectively as large-scale organizations (Birnbaum, 1988; Rowley et al., 1997).

This volume suggests many avenues for advancing knowledge by connecting and combining innovative approaches and by addressing gaps through best practices. Higher education organizations often fail to see opportunities for applying learning strategies at multiple scales and thus fail to amplify the benefits. The following sections identify ways to take what works at smaller scales (such as the level of the student and classroom) and apply similar techniques at larger scales (across the faculty and institution, for instance) in order to facilitate organizational learning.

Student Learning.   In this volume, we've seen that immersive, experiential, and high-engagement activities can facilitate deep learning among students (Wawrzynski & Baldwin, Chapter 5). Such activities encourage students to connect and integrate what they learn from one setting to the next (Barber, Chapter 1). Innovative approaches—such as those involving civic engagement (Moore & Mendez, Chapter 3) and technology-assisted, "blended" learning (VanDerLinden, Chapter 7)—can help educators reach more students more effectively. They can also help address differences in students' learning styles (Kolb, 1984, 1998) and extend the benefits of learning beyond the walls of the traditional classroom (Kerr, 1995). This alone can have exponential benefits.

For instance, Christensen, Horn, and Johnson (2011) explain up to now textbooks have been written by people who adopted/fit/mastered the dominant learning style used by the particular discipline. Students successful in this hegemonic mode of thinking are encouraged to enter the given field and ultimately replicate similar modes of teaching and learning. This pattern galvanizes the group, but also limits the breadth of perspectives held. Challenging the status quo promotes learning (Christensen et al., 2011). Using technology to adjust delivery, in order to convey content more effectively to a wider array of learners, can strengthen human capacity to address pressing challenges. New technologies also offer new ways to help individuals, organizational units, and institutions integrate learning that is happening in discrete areas (by blending and connecting them, for instance).

In addition, innovative strategies like those discussed in this volume can help institutions explain and justify their existence. The tactics can help higher education address public demands for accountability, for more-clearly articulated learning outcomes, and for higher graduation rates. All of these demands equate to ensuring higher return on investment (Leslie, Chapter 4 of this volume). "Scaling up" effective innovations can help society get more value from its expenditures. Promising innovations include tools to help various stakeholder groups integrate what they learn into wider and more diverse settings.

For students, learning-rich environments that provide fodder for "connection, application, and synthesis" (Barber, Chapter 1 of this volume) of new knowledge involve: classroom learning, cocurricular activities, internships, service learning/civic engagement projects (Moore & Mendez, Chapter 3 of this volume), blended learning (VanDerLinden, Chapter 7 of this volume), and other immersive experiences (Wawrzynski & Baldwin, Chapter 5 of this volume). Today, educators seek to make classrooms into immersive, high-impact environments by using techniques such as experiential learning and group-based discovery. These are the same characteristics undergirding cocurricular activities that make them so effective in fostering student development.

Student Learning Groups.   Scholars around the globe have shown group learning to be an effective way to foster students' development (Xiangyun, de Graaff, & Kolmos, 2009; Yadav, Subedi, Lundeberg, & Bunting, 2011).. Such techniques are associated with descriptors like student-centered, group-based, enquiry-driven, project-based, and/or problem-based learning. These pedagogical strategies encourage critical thinking and knowledge sharing. They also promote knowledge generation. Educators can use these pedagogies to help students integrate what they learn in various subjects and what they experience through many types of activities (Barber, Chapter 1 of this volume). All of these techniques have been shown to facilitate development of the orthogonal skills described by Leslie (Chapter 4 of this volume). An example of an orthogonal approach in practice occurs for engineering students at DIT, where target skills include: self-directed learning (SDL), creativity, critical thinking, information literacy, and ethics. In this program, the development of group skills is primary. It serves as a foundation for the development of all other disciplinary and nondisciplinary (e.g., personal) knowledge and skills. As is typical in Europe, students in this program do not take general education courses. Their technical courses must provide the general knowledge and skills necessary for them to succeed in their chosen profession and in life. Over time, direction from the teacher decreases, as students develop aptitude in guiding their own learning. As this happens, instructors' attention shifts toward helping students improve the quality of the products produced. Objectives, instructional methods, and assessment are aligned. They emphasize process in the early years and product later on.

One increasingly common method for structuring group-based learning among students is called problem-based learning (PBL). This hands-on approach, derived from medical education, places the individual's learning at the fore. Teachers serve as tutors or facilitators; they provide a framework around which students can construct new knowledge.

As codified by Barrows (1994), problem-based learning occurs in small groups (often 6–10 people). A problem—typically a fuzzy, ill-defined, and open-ended one—serves as the vehicle for learning. A teacher or facilitator helps guide the group, primarily serving as a tutor. This person unobtrusively advises the group with regard to learning and decision-making processes so that participants become increasingly effective in directing their own learning processes. The focus of the process is for group members to be the drivers of their own learning.

Faculty Learning.   Now, let's shift from considering self-directed learning at the student level to thinking about how it applies to faculty members and organizations. In doing so, we will see that learning theories are highly transferable from one stakeholder group to another. Later we will see that by combining and cross-referencing the learning that occurs within stakeholder groups, we can foster deep, transformational learning at and across various levels. Leaders can encourage this to happen by putting structures in place that facilitate integration. In this way, leaders can serve to pollinate ideas and germinate innovations that blossom up around them.

One type of immersive experience that has power to elicit deep learning for faculty and students alike is study abroad. International experiences can be just as important to faculty learning (Eddy, Chapter 2 of this volume) as they are for student learning (Lewis & Niesenbaum, 2005; NAFSA, 2003, 2006). Immersion and active engagement are integral to learning. Reflection can extend the benefits of participating in such programs (Astin, 1999). Prompting travelers to reflect on their experiences (as Eddy did) helps generate more knowledge than the experience alone would (sans reflection). Similarly, VanDerLinden (Chapter 7 of this volume) encourages institutional leaders to engage in this type of "critical self-reflection" (p. 83) about organizational learning.

A big takeaway from this volume is that traditional ways of teaching must be supplemented by new methods of learning and sharing knowledge. We can't rely solely on time-tested pedagogies like study abroad. Getting the most value for every dollar is particularly important in today's budgetary climate (Leslie, Chapter 4 of this volume). With less money available for faculty development programs, it becomes increasingly important to provide fun, enticing, and effective, low-cost ways to enrich faculty members' experiences and facilitate continual learning (Zakrajsek, Chapter 6 of this volume). Despite (or perhaps because of) the lack of funds for travel and other highly visible professional development programs, much of the onus for continued learning now falls on the individual faculty member. Zakrajsek challenges individual educators to take initiative, identify good sources of knowledge, and engage with others around campus. Tapping into the wealth of faculty and staff expertise can foster engagement and provide a ready sense of connection and fulfillment. It can help faculty integrate their own learning too (Barber, Chapter 1 of this volume).

Such action requires extra effort, but moving out of one's comfort zone is key to positive growth and development (Sanford, 1962). Facing unfamiliar situations prompts learning. Finding new environments for learning outside one's box is an underlying theme of Eddy's chapter (Chapter 2 of this volume), which describes how the move to another country can disrupt one's status quo and spark learning. International study programs, while costly, yield untold benefits for the faculty and students fortunate enough to participate (and for society as a whole, according to NAFSA, 2003, 2006). The effect of such programs can be amplified by including requirements for civic engagement (Moore & Mendez, Chapter 3 of this volume) as the Fulbright program does (Eddy, Chapter 2 of this volume). A primary benefit of such programs is development of the orthogonal skills (Leslie, Chapter 4 of this volume).

Faculty Learning Groups.   Groups of faculty and administrators can learn to self-direct their own learning. This process can enhance their capacity to generate knowledge, improve performance, and benefit from their own experiences. They can use the constructivist PBL approach defined by Barrows (1994), as happened at DIT. There, an administrator who was experienced with PBL guided lecturers through a process of self-directed learning. The faculty learning group identified its core "problem" as finding ways to facilitate group work among students and to assess students fairly.

Groups as Generators for Organizational Learning.   In the United States, a number of faculty groups have identified environmental sustainability as a core problem for investigation. Environmental sustainability is a pressing, open-ended issue where neither "the problem" nor "the solution" is readily apparent. Northern Arizona University (Chase & Rowland, 2005), Oberlin College (2013), and Harvard University (Sharp, 2009) provide vibrant examples of environmental learning that has occurred across stakeholder groups.

Through the Ponderosa Project at Northern Arizona University (NAU) faculty, staff, and students worked together to generate new systems, behaviors, and approaches to achieving environmental sustainability (Chase & Rowland, 2005). This particular university also provides the context for VanDerLinden's (Chapter 7 of this volume) discussion of blended learning. It appears that NAU consistently uses emerging challenges and technologies to promote active engagement and multilevel learning.

Likewise, events at Oberlin College reflect increased learning across stakeholder groups. Starting in 1992, David Orr (2007) began working with student groups to investigate environmental problems related to building design. Serving as a facilitator, he and his students followed a process similar to the one outlined by Barrows (1994). They identified opportunities, needs, where to get information, and how to apply it. They worked with architectural consultants to program a new building for their campus—an environmental studies center—that was not only built, but also came to serve as a precedent for the design of thousands more buildings around the world. The college has started to create new learning loops that draw from and extend what the student–faculty learning groups discovered/developed/generated.

Likewise, Harvard University is creating knowledge about sustainable construction in ways that involve multiple stakeholder groups and improve their buildings' performance (President and Fellows of Harvard College, 2009, 2010). The university is taking a systems-thinking perspective to engage various groups and to understand better the intersections of learning among stakeholders (Sharp, 2009).

NAU, Oberlin, and Harvard illustrate that learning that occurs among faculty and students has the potential to inform larger systems and address pressing social concerns. Institutional leaders are charged with ensuring that happens.

NEW DIRECTIONS FOR HIGHER EDUCATION • DOI: 10.1002/he

Learning Among Leaders.   On most campuses, group learning is not yet being tapped to its full potential by faculty and administrators. Nevertheless, these leaders are the stakeholders who can most affect knowledge generation at the organizational level, where new methods of learning from experience are highly desirable (Bornstein, 2003; Neumann & Bolitzer, Chapter 9 of this volume). Authors included in this volume have discussed the importance of organizational learning (Amey, Chapter 8; Moore & Mendez, Chapter 3; VanDerLinden, Chapter 7; Wawrzynski & Baldwin, Chapter 5). Their texts provide keys to helping postsecondary institutions learn more effectively. They can help us understand emerging techniques to address existing deficits. Their ideas can help leaders seize opportunities for growth and productivity.

Many of the techniques for organizational learning discussed in this volume were initially developed to facilitate learning by students and faculty. Moore and Mendez (Chapter 3 of this volume) and VanDerLinden (Chapter 7 of this volume) suggest ways to harness strategies that have worked at the level of the student/classroom and use them to facilitate organizational learning. One particularly valuable and highly transferrable approach is group-driven problem-based learning.

Like students, faculty and administrative leaders are learners. Faculty members also are decision makers who can, and should, put in place the structures needed to ensure high-impact learning across the domains for students. Administrative leaders must facilitate this work. Moreover, leaders are charged to create structures that facilitate high-impact learning across the domains *for faculty as well as for students.* In other words, leaders must create opportunities for faculty learning. In this regard, Neumann and Bolitzer's (Chapter 9) chapter highlights what leaders should be doing and what they need to know to get it done. "Leaders are usually better positioned," they say "to see and to explore group-level learning than are other organizational members" (p. 103).

Learning From Groups at DIT

DIT takes learning so seriously that the institution employs a "head of learning development" for each college who works with his/her dean to facilitate multidimensional, multiloop learning. Below, I provide two models to illustrate how multilevel learning unfolded at DIT. These models can help leaders visualize ways to build momentum within and between various constituent groups in order to prompt deep, transformational learning.

A Model for Multilevel Learning.   DIT showcases a model of multiloop learning. Here, group discovery served as the primary driver of transformational learning among individuals and the overall organization. At DIT today, more and more lecturers are implementing innovative PBL pedagogies. Even faculty who were initially skeptical about the approach or resistant to change are seeing benefits and altering their behaviors.

New Directions for Higher Education • DOI: 10.1002/he

Figure 10.1. Model for Multilevel Learning

Individual Learning   >>   Group Learning   >>   Organizational Learning

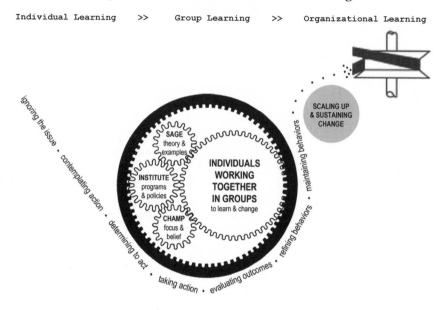

The institution provides resources to facilitate hands-on problem-based learning by individuals and groups. Today, efforts are underway to scale up, sustain, and help direct transformational learning. First, let's look at the core mechanism driving learning/change, in this case the faculty learning group, shown in the center of Figure 10.1, and then discuss how the system engaged more individuals (shown moving across the diagram from left to right) and began working to learn from members' experiences at the organizational level (shown on the upper right).

Group Learning.   At DIT, one group of faculty so valued the development of students' general, nondisciplinary skills that they met formally throughout the 2009–2010 school year to discuss how to use student learning groups to facilitate orthogonal development of such skills. Their discussions focused on ways to facilitate group learning, provide effective feedback to students, and assess (in a fair way) students working in groups. They developed ideas, tested the ideas in various classroom and laboratory settings, and met to share/reflect upon/refine the results. A study of the faculty learning group identified four key drivers that were effectively aligned to facilitate movement in the desired direction (Chance, Duffy, et al., 2013). Primary drivers were: (a) *individuals working together* in groups to learn and change, (b) *institutional programs and policies* to support learning,

(c) *a champion* who provided focus and belief related to an issue valued by the institution, and (d) *a sage adviser* who had a great deal of experience in the area where change was desired.

These four key elements worked together to draw more and more people into learning about and implementing the desired innovations (see Figure 10.1). Over time, leaders who desired to sustain the changes and help direct and scale-up the benefits saw the need to study and understand what happened.

The most crucial of the drivers was the group of individual faculty members working together to learn and change. The institution provided them with essential capacity-building programs, a policy requiring all incoming faculty members to earn credentials in learning and teaching, and incentives to help them utilize development programs. Incentives included awards, fellowships, faculty enrichment grants, tuition-remission, and course-release time. The institution also provided time for an administrative sage (a head of learning development) and a faculty champion (who was awarded a teaching fellowship) to organize activities. These individuals led what became a small movement that grew into a noteworthy transformation in teaching practices. Yet, as the model illustrates, neither the champion nor the sage could directly move the larger wheel of change. Instead, they affected change by engaging with others and leveraging institutional resources.

Individual Learning.   Initial resistance to change shifted as more individuals adopted the desired learning behaviors and practices. Individual teachers learned a range of new skills and behaviors. Consistent with the behavioral change model by Prochaska and DiClemente (1984), some individuals were initially unaware that change was needed/merited. This can range from a simple lack of awareness to denial of a need to change and/or active resistance. When things began to challenge that initial perception, a person began to contemplate action, determine to act, and take action to change or learn a new behavior. If the person is well-supported, s/he may be able to take this further: evaluating outcomes, refining behaviors, and maintaining the changes. Learning with a group can help; having an established place and time to reflect upon and discuss outcomes with others allows the learner to consider alternative approaches and hear about what worked in other contexts.

Organizational Learning.   In optimal cases leaders help mobilize, implement, and institutionalize change (Kezar, 2009). Mobilization of new approaches, according to VanDerLinden (Chapter 7 of this volume), involves "providing vision and harnessing enthusiasm" (p. 77) whereas implementation requires putting proper process and structures in place. Thus, the final stage of most models of planning/learning deals with monitoring, evaluating, and stabilizing desired changes. Individual teachers and students must monitor, perfect, and maintain their own teaching and learning practices.

Figure 10.2. Factors Driving Adoption of Learning/Change

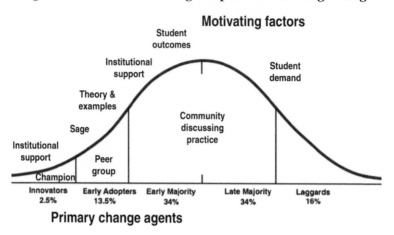

Organizations must provide resources to foster and sustain the new behaviors. Leaders must help channel activities so that energies flow in desired directions.

A Model to Promote Adoption.   Above is a model (see Figure 10.2) that provides a way to conceptualize the process of learning and change. Leaders can use it to help encourage adoption of new techniques by a critical mass (e.g., the early and late majority that represent the bulk of any given population).

Typically, the champion serves as the innovator who leverages the work of early adopters of new pedagogical practices. The learning/development can be enhanced by institutional support (in the form of policies and programs) and engagement of a sage adviser who can highlight relevant theories and examples, as was the case at DIT. Over time, more join the process to create the early majority, with the addition of the late majority buying in as they see improved student outcomes and increased student demand.

Lowe (2012) says leaders of socially driven enterprise should not waste precious resources trying to enlist laggards (who he defines as bystanders and naysayers). Rather, organizations will benefit most from recruiting skeptics who typically fall at the center of this bell curve. Moreover, Lowe says, leaders can yield the highest return on investment by helping "ensure the people who are using the solution are leveraging it to the maximum" (para. 8). Leaders should focus on helping constituents fully comprehend new approaches and learn to implement them effectively.

Leadership for Learning.   As found in the DIT research, faculty learning can foster—and is indeed central to—organizational learning

(Chance, Duffy, et al., 2013; Chance, Eddy, Duffy, Bowe, & Harvey, 2013). Any institution that wants to improve student learning will need faculty buy-in. Universities rely on faculty learning in order to achieve changes in teaching practices.

The example of DIT reflects best practices noted elsewhere in this volume. There, change was framed as a scholarly act that resulted in the willing engagement of faculty (Moore & Mendez, Chapter 3). The models provided above helped map the institution's learning environment as recommended by Wawrzynski and Baldwin (Chapter 5). Faculty members were engaged in critical reflection about how to achieve optimal learning (VanDerLinden, Chapter 7). In keeping with suggestions by Moore and Mendez (Chapter 3 of this volume), the faculty in the learning group at DIT effectively modeled "reflexive practice" about "how students at their institution engage and the outcomes of this engagement" (p. 36). The work helped constituents become more conscious and purposeful in their learning. As a result of this reflection, practices that support learning become more "embedded in the systems, structures, routines, practices, and strategies" (VanDerLinden, Chapter 7, p. 77) of the institution and its various programs.

Consistent with Amey's (Chapter 8 of this volume) recommendations, leaders in the organization helped construct a "learning infrastructure" of "support systems that foster people's willingness to take risks and learn" (p. 92). The system effectively provided "the space for thinking, reflecting, trying on new ideas, transitions, internalizing new understandings, and institutionalizing new processes" (p. 91). These factors helped build success and expand the group of educators facilitating change.

Summary

Although many chapters in this volume focus on learning within specific stakeholder groups (i.e., student, or faculty, or administrative leaders), there are clear commonalities. The examples provided in this chapter highlight a number of ways learning can occur across various stakeholder groups. All these groups can benefit from iterative thinking and from being exposed to heuristic processes for planning, decision making, and self-directed learning (Chance, 2010). They all need to know how to set benchmarks for success, monitor and evaluate their actions, and tweak their performance/behaviors.

Disrupting their status quo, while providing appropriate levels of challenge and support, can help them learn and grow (Sanford, 1962). Disruptive thinking is essential to spurring paradigm shifts (Kuhn, 1962) and to moving organizations from "good" to "great" (Collins & Hansen, 2011). In fact, Christensen and asscoiates (2011) argue that disruptive technologies will radically transform learning at all levels; this will help humanity develop knowledge much more effectively.

Using the models provided in this chapter can help institutional leaders leverage resources and prompt learning. They can implement capacity-building programs, empower champions and sage advisers, and work to align efforts for maximum effect. In cases where faculty members are already driving change, administrative leaders can and must help guide the change by providing essential resources. To maximize benefits, effective leaders will help scale up and sustain desired change. When this is done well, it can lead the organization in entirely new directions and can help define the institution's own unique role in education (Rowley et al., 1997).

References

Astin, A. W. (1999, September/October). Student involvement: A developmental theory for higher education. *Journal of College Student Development, 40*(5), 518–529.

Barrows, H. (1994). *Practice-based learning: Problem based learning applied to medical education.* Springfield: Southern Illinois School of Medicine.

Birnbaum, R. (1988). *How colleges work: The cybernetics of academic organization and leadership.* San Francisco, CA: Jossey-Bass.

Bornstein, R. (2003). *Legitimacy in the academic presidency: From entrance to exit.* Westport, CT: Praeger.

Chance, S. M. (2010). Strategic by design: Iterative approaches to educational planning. *Planning for Higher Education, 38*(2), 40–54.

Chance, S. M., Duffy, G., Bowe, B., Murphy, M., & Duggan, T. (2013, September). *A model for transforming engineering education through group learning.* Proceedings of the International Conference on Engineering and Product Design Education, Dublin, Ireland.

Chance, S. M., Eddy, P. L., Duffy, G., Bowe, B., & Harvey, J. (2013, June). *Policies that enhance learning and teaching.* Proceedings of the World Academy of Science, Engineering and Technology; International Conference on Higher Education, Paris, France.

Chase, G. W., & Rowland, P. (2005). The Ponderosa Project: Infusing sustainability in the curriculum. In P. F. Bartlett & G. W. Chase (Eds.), *Sustainability on campus: Stories and strategies for change* (pp. 91–105). Cambridge, MA: MIT Press.

Christensen, C. M., Horn, M. B., & Johnson, C. W. (2011). *Disrupting class: How disruptive innovation will change the way the world learns.* New York, NY: McGraw-Hill.

Collins, J., & Hansen, M. T. (2011). *Great by choice: Uncertainty, chaos, and luck—Why some survive despite them all.* New York, NY: HarperCollins.

Holcomb, E. L. (2001). *Asking the right questions* (2nd ed.). Thousand Oaks, CA: Corwin Press.

Kerr, C. (1995). *The uses of the university* (4th ed.). Cambridge, MA: Harvard University Press.

Kezar, A. (2005). What campuses need to know about organizational learning and the learning organization. In A. Kezar (Ed.), *New Directions for Higher Education: No. 131. Organizational learning in higher education* (pp. 7–22). San Francisco, CA: Jossey-Bass.

Kezar, A. (2009, January). *Synthesis of scholarship on change in higher education.* Paper presented at Mobilizing STEM Education for a Sustainable Future, Emory University, Atlanta, GA.

Kolb, D. A. (1984). *Experiential learning: Experience as the source of learning and development.* Englewood Cliffs, NJ: Prentice Hall.

Kolb, D. A. (1998). Learning styles and disciplinary differences. In K. A. Feldman & M. B. Paulsen (Eds.), *Teaching and learning in the college classroom* (pp. 127–137). Needham Heights, MA: Simon & Schuster.

Kuhn, T. (1962). *The structure of scientific revolutions.* Chicago, IL: University of Chicago.

Lauer, L. (2006). *Advancing higher education in uncertain times*. Washington, DC: Council for Advancement and Support of Education.

Lewis, T. L., & Niesenbaum, R. A. (2005, June 3). The benefits of short-term study abroad. *The Chronicle of Higher Education*. Retrieved from http://chronicle.com/article /The-Benefits-of-Short-Term/22274

Lowe, G. (2012, January 4). *For enterprise social networks: How much adoption is enough?* Retrieved from http://blog.yammer.com/blog/2012/01/how-much -adoption.html

NAFSA. (2003, November). *Securing America's future: Report of the strategic task force on education abroad*. Washington, DC: Author. Retrieved from http://www.nafsa.org /Resource_Library_Assets/Public_Policy/Securing_America_s_Future/

NAFSA. (2006, July 27). *Legislation introduced to dramatically expand study abroad among American college students; Bill proposes visionary program to ensure Americans are internationally educated*. NAFSA press release. Retrieved from http://www.nafsa.org /PressRoom/PressRelease.aspx?id=2134

Oberlin College. (2013). *Oberlin sustainability*. Retrieved from http://new.oberlin .edu/office/environmental-sustainability/index.dot

Orr, D. W. (2007). Ecological design and education. In J. Pretty, A. S. Ball, T. Benton, J. S. Guivant, D. R. Lee, D. Orr, M. J. Pfeffer, & H. Ward (Eds.), *The SAGE handbook of environment and society* (pp. 209–223). Los Angeles, CA: Sage.

President and Fellows of Harvard College. (2009). *Harvard receives 20th LEED certification*. Retrieved from http://green.harvard.edu/news/harvard-receives-20th -leed-certification

President and Fellows of Harvard College. (2010). *Fine arts library receives LEED gold certification*. Retrieved from http://www.hcl.harvard.edu /news/articles/2010/leed_certification.cfm

Presley, J. B., & Leslie, D. W. (1999). Understanding strategy: An assessment of theory and practice. In J. C. Smart & W. G. Tierney (Eds.), *Higher education: Handbook of theory and research* (Vol. 14, pp. 201–239). Bronx, NY: Agathon Press.

Prochaska, J. O., & DiClemente, C. C. (1984). *The transtheoretical approach: Crossing traditional boundaries of therapy*. Homewood, IL: Dow Jones-Irwin.

Rowley, D. J., Lujan, H. D., & Dolence, M. G. (1997). *Strategic change in colleges and universities: Planning to survive and prosper*. San Francisco, CA: Jossey-Bass.

Sanford, N. (1962). *The American college*. New York, NY: Wiley.

Sharp, L. (2009). Higher education: The quest for the sustainable campus. *Sustainability: Science, Practice, and Policy*, *1*(5), 1–7.

Wilson, D. (1997). Project monitoring: A newer component of the educational planning process. *Educational Planning*, *11*(1), 31–40.

Xiangyun, D., de Graaff, E., & Kolmos, A. (Eds.). (2009). *Research on PBL practice in engineering education*. Rotterdam, The Netherlands: Sense.

Yadav, A., Subedi, D., Lundeberg, M. A., & Bunting, C. F. (2011). Problem-based learning: Influence on students' learning in an electrical engineering course. *Journal of Engineering Education*, *100*(2), 253–280.

SHANNON M. CHANCE *is an associate professor of architecture at Hampton University, Hampton, VA.*

Index

HE 164 **Developing and Assessing Personal and Social Responsibility in College**

Robert D. Reason

In 2007, wanting to expand higher education's civic engagement conversation beyond voting behaviors, the Association of American Colleges and Universities launched the Core Commitments Initiative. That initiative focused attention on personal and social responsibility as outcomes of a college education, with the understanding that such a focus would return American higher education to its historical purpose of preparing active and engaged citizens. Expanding the conversation this way leaves room for behavioral measures, like voting or hours spent in community service, but also opens our understanding of citizenship to include issues of civic identity, civic attitudes, personal integrity, and ethics. This volume explores the research and practice related to the development of personal and social responsibility in college, drawing data directly from institutions that were part of the Core Commitments Initiative and providing instructive examples of good practice at both the programmatic and institutional levels.
ISBN: 978-1-1188-2805-2

HE 163 **Increasing Diversity in Doctoral Education: Implications for Theory and Practice**

Karri A. Holley, Joretta Joseph

Diversity is defined as those numerous elements of difference between groups of people that play significant roles in social institutions, including (but not limited to) race and ethnicity, gender, socioeconomic class, sexual orientation, and culture. Since doctoral degree recipients go on to assume roles as faculty and educators, diversity in doctoral programs is significant. By supporting graduate diversity across the academic disciplines, universities ensure that the nation's intellectual capacities and opportunities are fully realized. The authors of this volume consider diversity broadly from multiple perspectives, from race and ethnicity to institutional type, academic discipline, and national origin. Our intent is to demonstrate how diversity operates through these venues and definitions, and our hope is to stimulate a conversation about a key aspect of American higher education.
ISBN: 978-1-1187-8358-0

HE 162 **Collegiate Transfer: Navigating the New Normal**

Janet L. Marling

Although students have been moving between institutions and attempting to import credit for many years, current data show that transfer is becoming an increasingly common approach to higher education. This volume is dedicated to exploring this new normal and has been written with a broad constituency in mind. It is intended to assist institutions, higher education agencies, and even state legislative bodies as they navigate the challenges of serving transfer students, a

diverse, integral segment of our higher education system. Most available research has explored the two-year to four-year transfer track, and the practical examples provided here often use that framework. However, real-world transition issues are not restricted to a specific higher education sector, and readers interested in the sometimes complex processes of other transfer pathways will gain valuable insight as well.
ISBN: 978-1-1187-0102-7

HE 161 Reframing Retention Strategy for Institutional Improvement

David H. Kalsbeek

In the midst of the vast collection of work that already exists on student retention, this volume addresses the apparent difficulty in gaining traction at the institutional level in improving student retention and degree completion rates—especially at larger fouryear institutions where size, complexity, and multiplicity of structures and processes present particular challenges. This volume offers a way for institutional leaders to better focus their time, energy, and resources in their retention effort by framing the way they think about it using the 4 Ps of retention strategy: *profile, progress, process,* and *promise.* This simple framework challenges long-standing, traditional assumptions about student retention that can distract and dilute institutional efforts, and helps keep those efforts sharply and singularly focused on improving retention and degree completion outcomes.

HE 160 Codes of Conduct in Academia

John M. Braxton, Nathaniel J. Bray

Chapters of this issue of New Directions for Higher Education present tenets of codes of conduct for the presidency, academic deans, admissions officers, fund-raising professionals, faculty who teach undergraduate students, and faculty who teach graduate students. The need for such codes of conduct stems from the client-serving role of colleges and universities. Such clients include prospective donors, prospective students and their families, the individual college or university, faculty members, undergraduate and graduate students, and the knowledge base of the various academic disciplines. Because presidents, academic deans, admissions officers, fund-raising professionals, and faculty members experience role ambiguity and substantial autonomy in the performance of their roles, codes of conduct are needed to protect the welfare of the clients served. The authors offer recommendations for policy and practice regarding the proposed codes of conduct. Organizational constraints and possibilities of enacting such codes are also discussed.
ISBN: 978-1-1185-3775-6

HE 159 In Transition: Adult Higher Education Governance in Private Institutions

J. Richard Ellis, Stephen D. Holtrop

Adult degree programs can pose challenges to traditional campus structures. This volume of case studies shows a number of small, independent universities addressing various administrative and service functions for their adult programs. Institutions have unique internal structures and distinctive histories, which mean some adult programs remain very connected to the central campus administrative and

service functions while others develop autonomy in a number of areas. As an adult program grows, its relationship with the traditional program changes, while outside forces and internal reevaluation of priorities and finances also work to realign the balance of centralized and autonomous functions. Balancing these functions in an institution-specific hybrid structure can provide both a measure of autonomy and centralized efficiency and consistency. In the end, each institution needs to find its own balance of centralized and decentralized services and administrative functions. Mutual appreciation and collaboration are keys to finding such an institutional balance.
ISBN: 978-1-1184-7749-6

HE 158 Dual Enrollment: Strategies, Outcomes, and Lessons for School–College Partnerships

Eric Hofmann, Daniel Voloch
In order to achieve the ambitious national goal of increasing the number of college graduates over the next decade, high schools and postsecondary institutions must collaborate more intentionally to help students become college ready. This volume focuses on the goals, practices, policies, and outcomes of programs that enroll high school students in college courses for college credit. Referred to as dual enrollment programs, these opportunities support students' transition to, and success in, college.

This volume of New Directions for Higher Education presents quantitative and qualitative studies that investigate the impact of dual enrollment programs on student and faculty participants. Accounts by dual enrollment program administrators provide examples of how their programs operate and how data have been used to set benchmarks for program success. Chapters also explore models that build off dual enrollment's philosophy of school–college partnerships and embrace a more robust framework for supporting college transition, including the development of early colleges and a new approach to community college design in New York City.

Dual enrollment inhabits a place where practitioners confront significant questions with regard to higher education on a seemingly daily basis. The collection of researchers and practitioners gathered here examine the details of dual enrollment programs, their impact on student achievement and institutional practices, and the role of higher education in improving K–12 education.
ISBN: 978-1-1184-0523-9

NEW DIRECTIONS FOR HIGHER EDUCATION

ORDER FORM SUBSCRIPTION AND SINGLE ISSUES

DISCOUNTED BACK ISSUES:

Use this form to receive 20% off all back issues of *New Directions for Higher Education.*
All single issues priced at **$23.20** (normally $29.00)

TITLE	ISSUE NO.	ISBN

*Call 888-378-2537 or see mailing instructions below. When calling, mention the promotional code JBNND
to receive your discount. For a complete list of issues, please visit www.josseybass.com/go/ndhe*

SUBSCRIPTIONS: (1 YEAR, 4 ISSUES)

☐ New Order   ☐ Renewal

U.S.	☐ Individual: $89	☐ Institutional: $311
CANADA/MEXICO	☐ Individual: $89	☐ Institutional: $351
ALL OTHERS	☐ Individual: $113	☐ Institutional: $385

*Call 888-378-2537 or see mailing and pricing instructions below.
Online subscriptions are available at www.onlinelibrary.wiley.com*

ORDER TOTALS:

Issue / Subscription Amount: $ _____

Shipping Amount: $ _____
(for single issues only – subscription prices include shipping)

Total Amount: $ _____

SHIPPING CHARGES:

First Item	$6.00
Each Add'l Item	$2.00

*(No sales tax for U.S. subscriptions. Canadian residents, add GST for subscription orders. Individual rate subscriptions must
be paid by personal check or credit card. Individual rate subscriptions may not be resold as library copies.)*

BILLING & SHIPPING INFORMATION:

☐ **PAYMENT ENCLOSED:** *(U.S. check or money order only. All payments must be in U.S. dollars.)*

☐ **CREDIT CARD:** ☐ VISA ☐ MC ☐ AMEX

Card number _____Exp. Date_____

Card Holder Name_____Card Issue # _____

Signature _____Day Phone _____

☐ **BILL ME:** *(U.S. institutional orders only. Purchase order required.)*

Purchase order # _____
Federal Tax ID 13559302 • GST 89102-8052

Name _____

Address_____

Phone_____ E-mail_____

Copy or detach page and send to: **John Wiley & Sons, One Montgomery Street, Suite 1200,
San Francisco, CA 94104-4594**

Order Form can also be faxed to: **888-481-2665**

PROMO JBNND